DEVON

Travel Guide

2024-2025

Exploring Coastal Charms, Embracing Countryside Retreats, and Unraveling Historic Marvels

JAMES GRAHAM

Copyright Page © 2024 by JAMES GRAHAM

All rights reserved. No part of this publication may be reproduced, distributed, or transmitted in any form or by any means, including photocopying, recording, or other electronic or mechanical methods, without the prior written permission the copyright holder, except in the case of brief quotations embodied in critical reviews and certain other noncommercial uses permitted by copyright law.

SCAN QR CODE WITH DEVICE TO GAIN ACCESS TO MORE OF MY BOOKS

TABLE OF CONTENTS

INTRODUCTION   7
FREQUENTLY ASKED QUESTIONS (FAQs)   9
CHAPTER 1
GETTING TO KNOW DEVON   13
   Geographic Overview   13
   Devon History   15
   Economy and Industries   18
   County Laws and Regulations   21
   Cultural Diversity   23

CHAPTER 2
PLANNING YOUR TRIP   27
   Best Time to Visit Devon   27
   Budgeting and Travel Costs   30
   Visa and Entry Requirements   34
   Travel Insurance and Health Preparations   37
   Packing Tips and Essentials   40

CHAPTER 3
EXPLORING THE REGIONS   43
   Regions of Devon   43
   Must-See Attractions   45
   Off-the-Beaten-Path Destinations   47

CHAPTER 4
ACCOMMODATIONS OPTIONS **49**
    Hotels and Resorts in Devon   49
    Charming Bed and Breakfast   56
    Camping and RV Options in Devon   59
    Vacation Rentals in Devon   63
    Hostels and Budget Accommodations   65

CHAPTER 5
FOOD AND DINING **69**
    Devon's Culinary Tapestry   69
    Popular Dishes and Local Specialties   73
    Best Restaurants and Dining Experiences   75
    Dietary Preferences and Restrictions   77

CHAPTER 6
TOURS AND ATTRACTIONS **81**
    Guided Tours and Excursions   81
    Historic Sites and Landmarks   87
    Museums and Art Galleries   90
    Entertainment and Nightlife   94

CHAPTER 7
OUTDOOR ADVENTURE AND NATURAL WONDERS **97**
    Hikes & Trails in Devon   97
    National and County Parks   100
    Water Activities in Devon.   102
    Wildlife Watching in Devon.   105
    Scenic Drives In Devon   107

CHAPTER 8
SHOPPING AND SOUVENIR   **111**
    Unique Devon Souvenirs   111
    Local Markets and Shopping Districts   113
    Crafts & Arts   114
    Antique Stores   116

CHAPTER 9
ITINERARY   **119**
    Short Stay Itinerary (2 Days)   119
    Medium Stay Itinerary (5 Days)   121
    Extended Stay Itinerary (10 Days)   125

CHAPTER 10
SAFETY, HEALTH TIPS, AND FIRST AID   **129**
    Travel Safety Tips   129
    Health Precautions   131
    Emergency Contacts   133
    First Aid Essentials   134

CONCLUSION   **138**

INTRODUCTION

Embark on an enthralling journey through Europe's heart with the "Devon Travel Guide." Devon, nestled in captivating landscapes, invites exploration with a rich tapestry of history, cultural marvels, traditions, and lively celebrations. Flip through the guidebook to envision cobblestone streets echoing tales of centuries past, each step resonating with a storied heritage.

Devon, steeped in history, reveals its narrative through medieval castles, ancient cathedrals, and timeless villages. Navigate its historical labyrinth, where every stone shares a story and every hillside holds a chapter waiting to be uncovered. Immerse in the cultural richness that graces this scenic landscape, where towns and hamlets stand as living legacies of generations.

This guide doesn't just recount history; it invites you to be a part of it. Experience Devon's warm hospitality as locals welcome you with open arms, ready to unveil the secrets of their cherished land. Let the aroma of traditional cuisine guide you on a culinary adventure, savoring flavors perfected over centuries. From cream teas in charming tea rooms to seaside savory pasties, Devon's gastronomic wonders will leave a lasting impression on your travel memories.

The journey extends beyond history and cuisine into Devon's vibrant festivals. Picture yourself amidst lively festivities, where locals and visitors unite to celebrate life, love, and laughter. Whether it's vibrant carnivals, valley-filling music festivals, or timeless traditions, Devon's festivals offer a kaleidoscope of joy, infusing your journey with unforgettable moments.

As you navigate the "Devon Travel Guide ," let it be your compass through this captivating landscape. Delve into Devon's soul, where each nuance is a brushstroke painting a masterpiece lingering in your heart. This guide transcends being a mere roadmap; it's an invitation to connect with a place that defies time, embarking on an odyssey beyond the ordinary. Welcome to Devon – where the past intertwines with the present, and every moment unfolds as an adventure.

FREQUENTLY ASKED QUESTIONS (FAQs)

I have shared useful tips for planning a trip to Devon. Always remember to research and keep updated with the latest travel requirements and conditions before your adventure.

1. What sets Devon apart as a distinctive European travel spot?
    - Devon's allure lies in its blend of rich history, scenic landscapes, and vibrant cultural traditions. Immerse yourself in medieval castles, charming villages, and a captivating heritage that distinguishes it from other European destinations.

2. Which historical sites are must-visits in Devon?
    - Uncover Devon's history by exploring landmarks like Dartmoor National Park, Powderham Castle, and Exeter Cathedral. Each site unfolds a captivating story, providing a window into the region's intriguing past.

3. What local dishes should I try in Devon?
    - Treat your taste buds to Devon's culinary gems, such as cream teas, pasties, and fresh seafood. The guide directs you to local

eateries for an authentic taste that defines Devon's gastronomic scene.

4. Are there unique customs or cultural nuances in Devon for visitors to be aware of?
- Gain insights into Devon's warm hospitality and cultural nuances, enhancing your interaction with locals. Learn about customs that reflect the region's identity and enrich your travel experience.

5. Which festivals offer an immersive experience in Devon?
- Immerse yourself in Devon's lively festival scene, featuring colorful carnivals, music festivals, and timeless traditions. The guide provides an event calendar, ensuring you partake in celebrations that add dynamic flair to your journey.

6. What outdoor activities are popular in Devon?
- Explore Devon's outdoor wonders, from hiking in Dartmoor to discovering the breathtaking coastline. Whether you're an adventure enthusiast or a nature lover, the guide offers activity recommendations catering to diverse interests.

7. How can I engage with the local community during my stay in Devon?
- Experience Devon's hospitality by joining community events, workshops, and interacting with locals. The guide provides insights on connecting with the community for a more enriching travel experience.

8. What transportation modes are best for exploring Devon?
- Receive practical tips on navigating Devon's landscapes, including recommendations for public transportation, car rentals, and convenient travel modes. The guide ensures efficient and comfortable exploration of the region.

9. Any hidden gems or off-the-beaten-path destinations in Devon?
- Venture beyond tourist hotspots and discover hidden gems showcasing Devon's authentic essence. The guide unveils lesser-known destinations, allowing you to experience the true spirit of the region.

10. How can I optimize my time in Devon?
- Receive expert advice on crafting an itinerary that maximizes your time in Devon. Whether a weekend or a week, the

guide provides suggestions for a well-rounded and fulfilling travel experience in this enchanting European destination.

CHAPTER 1
GETTING TO KNOW DEVON

Geographic Overview

Situated in the enchanting southwestern corner of England, Devon unfolds as a captivating masterpiece of diverse landscapes, creating an irresistible destination for both explorers and nature enthusiasts. Bordered by Cornwall to the west, Somerset to the northeast, and the English Channel to the south, Devon stands out as a quintessential retreat, offering a harmonious blend of tranquility and adventure.

Landscapes and Terrain
Devon's topography is a testament to nature's artistry, displaying an extraordinary variety that paints the quintessence of England's countryside.

Vast moorlands, rolling hills, and verdant valleys form a vibrant patchwork of colors and textures. Dartmoor National Park, a symbol of rugged beauty, features granite tors, ancient standing stones, and meandering rivers. To the north, Exmoor National Park boasts dramatic cliffs meeting the sea and hidden valleys preserving untouched wilderness.

Coastline and Beaches

Devon's coastline is a poetic canvas of natural wonders. The UNESCO-listed Jurassic Coast unfolds along the southern edge, revealing ancient rock formations, fossil-rich beaches, and towering cliffs. Sandy shores and secluded coves invite strolls, while coastal towns like Salcombe and Sidmouth add maritime charm with their colorful houses overlooking the azure waters of the English Channel.

Rivers and Valleys

Devon's rivers contribute to its fertility and picturesque allure. The River Exe, Dart, and Tamar carve valleys nurturing lush meadows and providing a cradle for traditional farming. The Tamar Valley, an Area of Outstanding Natural Beauty, harmonizes rolling hills and meandering waterways, creating a haven for wildlife and a retreat for those seeking serenity.

Wildlife and Conservation

Devon's geographical diversity shelters a rich array of wildlife, making it a haven for naturalists. Dartmoor's open spaces host the iconic Dartmoor ponies, and coastal cliffs become bustling seabird colonies. Conservation efforts, especially in the South Devon Area of Outstanding Natural Beauty, emphasize preserving unique habitats, ensuring a sustainable coexistence between humans and the natural world.

Climate and Weather

Devon's temperate maritime climate adds allure to its geographical makeup, featuring mild winters and warm summers. The proximity to the Atlantic Ocean moderates temperatures, creating an inviting environment for year-round exploration. This climate, conducive to vibrant flora and fauna, enhances the allure of the county.

Devon History

Embark on a captivating journey through time as we unveil Devon's rich history—a tapestry woven with tales of ancient civilizations, maritime exploits, and cultural evolution. Rooted in the annals of England's history, Devon's heritage spans millennia, leaving indelible marks on the landscapes and communities that grace this timeless region.

Prehistoric Marvels

Devon's origins trace back to the Paleolithic era, when human habitation left a mark on the granite tors and moorlands of Dartmoor. Megalithic structures and burial sites bear witness to a complex prehistoric society, laying the foundation for the captivating story that unfolds across the ages.

Roman Footprints

Roman conquest embraced Devon, with Exeter, known as Isca Dumnoniorum, becoming a vital administrative center. Remnants of Roman architecture, such as city walls and baths in Exeter, provide glimpses into this period, marking the convergence of Roman influence and local history.

Anglo-Saxon Legacy

Post-Roman, the Anglo-Saxons shaped Devon's landscape, fostering centers of learning and religious activity in monasteries like Buckfast and Tavistock. The synthesis of Celtic and Saxon cultures defined the socio-cultural tapestry of the region.

Norman Conquest and Medieval Marvels

The Norman Conquest ushered in a new era with the construction of strategic castles like Exeter Castle. Feudal structures emerged, and medieval Devon witnessed the rise of market towns, trade, and the distinct regional identity that still resonates.

Maritime Brilliance

Devon's maritime prowess came to the forefront during the Age of Exploration. Native figures like Sir Walter Raleigh and Sir Francis Drake played pivotal roles, with Plymouth witnessing the historic departure of the Mayflower in 1620, carrying Pilgrims to the New World.

Industrial Revolution to Victorian Elegance

The Industrial Revolution left an indelible mark on Devon in the 18th and 19th centuries. Mining, railways, and canals transformed the landscape, and Victorian architecture, epitomized by Brunel's atmospheric railway in Torquay, became emblematic of progress.

World Wars and Post-War Transformation

Devon played a strategic role in both World Wars, shaping its coastal defenses. Post-war, urban development and tourism flourished, drawing visitors to the county's natural beauty. Coastal towns became hubs, marking the inception of Devon's modern tourism industry.

Cultural Tapestry

Devon's cultural contributions extend to literature, with luminaries like Agatha Christie finding inspiration in its landscapes. Rich folklore, brimming with tales of pixies and mythical creatures, has also left an indelible mark on literature and art.

Contemporary Charm

Today, Devon thrives as a dynamic county, seamlessly blending historical legacy with modern vibrancy. Historic landmarks coexist with modern cities, cultural festivals, and a commitment to environmental sustainability, creating a living testament to Devon's enduring spirit.

Economy and Industries

Devon's economic vibrancy mirrors the diversity of its landscapes and the resilience of its communities. Nestled between rural expanses and picturesque coastlines, the county's economic tapestry weaves together traditional sectors and emerging industries, creating a unique blend that defines Devon's economic character.

Agriculture and Farming

The fertile valleys and rolling hills of Devon have nurtured a robust agricultural sector. Renowned for dairy farming, particularly with the high-quality milk produced by Devon cattle, the county also thrives on sheep farming. Farmers' markets and agricultural fairs celebrate the bounty of Devon's fields, connecting the community with locally sourced produce.

Tourism and Hospitality

Devon's allure as a tourist destination contributes significantly to its economic landscape. Coastal resorts like Torquay and Exmouth beckon sun-seekers to pristine beaches, while heritage sites like Buckfast Abbey and Dartington Hall offer cultural experiences. The tourism sector, inclusive of hospitality and recreation, plays a pivotal role in shaping Devon's economy.

Maritime and Fishing

With an extensive coastline along the English Channel and the Atlantic Ocean, maritime industries have deep roots in Devon. Fishing communities in towns like Brixham contribute to the thriving seafood industry, while Plymouth engages in shipbuilding, marine engineering, and naval activities, showcasing the county's maritime heritage.

Renewable Energy
Devon is at the forefront of the renewable energy movement. Wind farms harness the power of southwest winds, aligning with the county's commitment to sustainability. Initiatives in solar energy and environmentally conscious practices further underscore Devon's dedication to responsible energy solutions.

Technology and Innovation
Recent years have witnessed the emergence of technology and innovation sectors in Devon. The county has become a hub for technology companies, particularly in software development and digital marketing. Innovation centers and research institutions collaborate to drive advancements, positioning Devon as a player in the ever-evolving tech landscape.

Arts and Crafts
Devon's rich cultural heritage finds expression in a vibrant arts and crafts scene. From traditional pottery in Bideford to contemporary art galleries in Exeter, the creative industries not only contribute to

the economy but also shape the cultural identity of the county.

Education and Research

Devon's intellectual capital is bolstered by the presence of universities and research institutions, including the esteemed University of Exeter. Research endeavors span fields like environmental science, marine biology, and sustainable development, fostering innovation and knowledge exchange.

County Laws and Regulations

Embarking on the exploration of Devon's beauty requires a grasp of the county's laws and regulations, crafted to ensure the safety, well-being, and harmonious coexistence of residents and visitors.

Traffic and Road Etiquette

Devon's scenic routes come with traffic and road regulations, ensuring safe and efficient travel. Be mindful of speed limits, parking rules, and road-specific guidelines. Adhering to these regulations ensures a seamless and enjoyable journey through the county's picturesque landscapes.

Environmental Stewardship

Preserving Devon's natural allure is a shared responsibility. Regulations promoting environmental conservation, especially in reserves and parks, emphasize Leave No Trace principles. Visitors play a crucial role in sustaining the diverse ecosystems that make Devon a sanctuary for wildlife and nature enthusiasts.

Heritage Respect:

Devon's historical treasures are safeguarded by regulations governing the preservation of listed buildings and archaeological sites. Understanding and respecting these regulations contribute to the ongoing efforts to protect and cherish the country's rich heritage.

Maritime and Coastal Guidelines

With an extensive coastline, maritime regulations prioritize safety and environmental protection. Visitors engaging in coastal activities should familiarize themselves with guidelines governing boating, fishing, and other maritime pursuits.

Public Order and Safety

Devon's regulations uphold public safety and orderly conduct. From events and gatherings to responsible alcohol consumption, compliance with these rules fosters a positive experience for both residents and visitors.

Hospitality Compliance

Accommodation regulations ensure safety and quality standards. Visitors staying in various accommodations should be aware of hospitality regulations, including licensing requirements and specific guidelines set by establishments.

Health and Safety Protocols

Given current global health concerns, health and safety regulations are crucial. Adhering to guidelines related to public health, food safety, and emergency protocols contributes to the well-being of the community.

Cultural Considerations

While not legal regulations, cultural sensitivity and respect for local customs are paramount. Appreciating Devon's diverse cultural heritage enhances interactions with the local community, fostering positive experiences for all.

Cultural Diversity

Devon's cultural identity is a vibrant mosaic woven from the threads of history, folklore, and the traditions of its diverse communities. This rich tapestry, shaped by centuries of influence, paints a portrait of warmth and inclusivity, inviting all to explore its unique heritage.

Indigenous Roots
The native communities of Devon, rooted in ancient history, form the bedrock of the county's cultural mosaic. Descendants of the Celts and Saxons have imprinted their traditions, language, and folklore on the local identity. Unique festivals and celebrations stand as living testaments to their enduring influence.

Maritime Legacy
Devon's cultural identity is deeply intertwined with its maritime history. Tales of sailors, explorers, and maritime legends echo in the coastal communities. Plymouth, a historic naval port, proudly bears witness to the county's seafaring legacy.

Artistic Inspiration
Devon's landscapes and coastal vistas have been a wellspring of inspiration for artists and writers. The county's scenic locales, immortalized by renowned crime novelist Agatha Christie and countless others, contribute to the vibrant artistic tapestry.

Festivals and Diversity

Devon's calendar is a lively canvas painted with festivals that showcase its cultural diversity. From the lively Orange Races in Totnes to the ancient traditions of the Abbotskerswell Worm Charming Festival, each event is a celebration of the uniqueness embedded in Devon's communities.

Culinary Fusion
Devon's culinary heritage is a delightful fusion of local produce and historical influences. From the iconic cream teas to hearty dishes like Devonshire pasties and saffron cake, the county's gastronomy is a reflection of its cultural diversity.

Language and Dialects
While English is the primary language, Devon retains distinct dialects and linguistic nuances that add to its cultural charm. Local sayings, expressions, and the unique Devon accent contribute to the linguistic diversity that defines the region.

Religious Heritage
Devon's religious heritage is etched in its historic churches, cathedrals, and monastic sites. Architectural marvels like the cathedrals in Exeter and Plymouth, alongside the serene Buckfast Abbey, stand as symbols of the county's spiritual legacy.

Contemporary Expressions

In harmony with its historical roots, Devon embraces contemporary cultural expressions. The county hosts a kaleidoscope of arts festivals, music events, and theater productions that bridge the gap between tradition and modernity, uniting diverse artists and audiences.

CHAPTER 2
PLANNING YOUR TRIP

Best Time to Visit Devon

Selecting the perfect time to explore Devon is akin to choosing from a trove of treasures, each season offering a distinct allure to captivate travelers. From the blossoming grace of spring to the cozy festivities of winter, Devon stands as a year-round destination, promising a tapestry of experiences.

Spring (March to May)
In spring, Devon's countryside undergoes a metamorphosis, adorned with vibrant hues. With temperatures ranging from 8°C to 15°C (46°F to 59°F), this season unveils blooming flowers and verdant landscapes. Dive into the rejuvenating spirit of Devon by strolling through historic gardens like

RHS Garden Rosemoor or exploring coastal paths adorned with wildflowers.

Signature Event:
- Devon County Show (May): Immerse yourself in agricultural splendor and local culture at one of the region's largest gatherings.

Summer (June to August)

Summer in Devon is a celebration of sunlit days and coastal enchantment. With temperatures from 15°C to 25°C (59°F to 77°F), the beaches along the English Riviera beckon, and coastal towns buzz with life. Seize the season for water adventures, leisurely coastal walks, and embracing the maritime essence that defines Devon.

Signature Events:
- Regatta Season (Various Locations): Immerse yourself in nautical festivities during regatta events.
- Torbay Airshow (June): Marvel at breathtaking aerial displays over the stunning Torbay coastline.

Autumn (September to November)

Autumn in Devon unveils a golden spectacle as temperatures range from 10°C to 18°C (50°F to

64°F). Ideal for exploring Dartmoor National Park amidst a palette of red and gold foliage. Food enthusiasts can relish the Dartmouth Food Festival, celebrating the gastronomic richness of the region.

Signature Event:
- Dartmouth Food Festival (October): Indulge in local produce and culinary delights against a picturesque backdrop.

Winter (December to February)
Devon's winter exudes tranquility, with temperatures ranging from 2°C to 10°C (36°F to 50°F). Experience the festive charm through Christmas markets in historic towns and cozy pubs with roaring fires. Unique New Year's Eve celebrations, like those in Clovelly, offer a distinctive way to welcome the new year.

Signature Events:
- Christmas Markets (Various Locations): Immerse yourself in the festive spirit with charming Christmas markets.
- Clovelly's New Year's Eve Celebrations: Embrace a traffic-free celebration in a historic village.

Overall Tips for the Best Time to Visit Devon

1. Shoulder Seasons: Opt for the spring or autumn shoulder seasons for pleasant weather and fewer crowds.

2. Event Planning: Check the local calendar for festivals aligning with your interests.

3. Accommodation: Secure accommodations well in advance, especially during peak summer months.

Budgeting and Travel Costs

Embarking on a journey through Devon's scenic landscapes doesn't have to be a financial challenge. Whether you're a thrifty traveler or one with a taste for luxury, Devon caters to diverse budgets. Here's a comprehensive guide to help you navigate accommodation, transportation, dining, and activities while keeping your budget intact.

Accommodation Costs

1. Budget-Friendly Options:
    - Hostels and Guesthouses: Affordable and comfortable stays for budget-conscious travelers.
    - Camping Sites: Embrace nature with budget-friendly campsites, ideal during warmer months.

2. Mid-Range Choices:
    - Bed and Breakfasts: Experience local hospitality without breaking the bank.
    - Country Inns: Quaint inns in the heart of Devon's countryside for a unique stay.

3. Luxurious Retreats:
    - Boutique Hotels: Indulge in luxury with boutique hotels, each offering a unique charm.
    - Coastal Resorts: Experience breathtaking views and top-notch amenities in popular destinations like Salcombe and Dartmouth.

Transportation Expenses

1. Public Transport:
    - Buses and Trains: Cost-effective public transport for exploring towns and cities.

- Travel Passes: Opt for regional travel passes for unlimited transportation within specific areas.

2. Car Rentals:
   - Renting a Car: Explore Devon at your own pace by renting a car. Compare prices to find the best deals.

3. Walking and Cycling:
   - Local Exploration: Save on transportation costs by walking or cycling in smaller towns and villages.

Dining and Food Costs

1. Local Markets and Street Food:
   - Farmers' Markets: Immerse yourself in Devon's culinary scene by visiting local farmers' markets.
   - Street Food: Relish regional specialties from street food vendors for a budget-friendly gastronomic adventure.

2. Pubs and Cafés:
   - Traditional Pubs: Enjoy affordable meals and a cozy atmosphere in traditional pubs.
   - Cafés: Opt for cafés with budget-friendly options, especially during lunch.

3. Fine Dining:
- Special Occasions: Allocate a budget for fine dining experiences, balancing luxury with cost-effective choices.
- Set Menus: Explore set menus or lunch specials at upscale restaurants for a more economical dining experience.

Activity and Sightseeing Costs

1. Free Attractions:
- Beaches and Coastal Walks: Explore the stunning coastline and beaches without spending a penny.
- Nature Reserves: Visit free-to-enter nature reserves for wildlife enthusiasts.

2. Paid Experiences:
- Historical Sites: Budget for entrance fees to historical sites and landmarks.
- Guided Tours: Invest in guided tours for a deeper exploration of Devon's rich history.

Overall Budgeting Tips

1. Off-Peak Travel:
- Accommodation: Consider off-peak seasons for potential discounts on accommodation.

- Activities: Some attractions offer reduced prices during off-peak times.

2. Accommodation Packages:
    - Bundled Deals: Explore accommodation bundles that include extras like breakfast or attraction tickets.

3. Local Markets:
    - Self-Catering: Save on meals by buying fresh produce from local markets and preparing some meals yourself.

Visa and Entry Requirements

Preparing for your journey to Devon involves understanding the visa and entry requirements to ensure a seamless and enjoyable experience. Devon, a gem in England's southwest, welcomes travelers from various corners of the globe. Here's a comprehensive guide to help you navigate the entry process:

European Union Citizens

1. Visa Exemption (Pre-Brexit):
    - Historically, citizens of European Union (EU) countries did not require a visa to enter

the UK, including Devon, due to visa-free travel agreements.

2. Post-Brexit Changes:
- Following Brexit, it's essential to stay updated on any changes in visa requirements. Regularly check the official UK government's website and consult your local embassy for the latest information.

Non-European Union Citizens

1. Visa Requirements:
- Citizens from non-EU countries may need a visa to enter the UK. Check the official UK government website or contact the nearest British embassy or consulate for up-to-date visa requirements.

2. Purpose and Duration:
- Visa requirements vary based on the purpose and duration of your visit (tourist, business, etc.). Ensure you have the correct visa category for a smooth entry into Devon.

Passport Requirements

1. Validity:
   - Check that your passport is valid for at least six months beyond your intended travel date.

Entry Process

1. Essential Documents:
   - Have the following documents ready for customs and immigration checks:
   - Passport with necessary stamps.
   - Valid visa (if applicable).
   - Evidence of return or onward travel plans.

COVID-19 Considerations

1. Travel Restrictions:
   - Stay informed about any COVID-19-related travel restrictions. Regularly check the official UK government's COVID-19 guidance website for updates.

2. Testing Requirements:
   - Be aware of pre-departure or on-arrival COVID-19 testing requirements. Ensure compliance with testing protocols, including presenting a negative test result if necessary.

3. Quarantine Regulations:
   - Understand quarantine regulations that may apply. Be prepared for the possibility of quarantine, especially when traveling from high-risk areas.

Travel Insurance and Health Preparations

Embarking on a trip to Devon comes with the excitement of exploring its captivating beauty. To guarantee a secure and worry-free experience, let's delve into the essentials – comprehensive travel insurance and health preparation tips.

Why Travel Insurance Matters

1. Medical Safety First:
   - Devon's allure comes with the responsibility of being ready for any medical situation. Travel insurance covers unforeseen medical emergencies, ensuring access to quality healthcare without financial stress.

2. Safeguarding Your Plans:
   - Unexpected circumstances might disrupt your trip plans. . Travel insurance protects your investment by covering trip

cancellations or delays caused by personal emergencies or unforeseen circumstances.

3. Guarding Your Belongings:
   - Protect against loss or theft of valuables with travel insurance. This includes passports, electronics, or luggage, allowing you to minimize potential losses.

4. Emergency Evacuations Covered:
   - In rare serious incidents, travel insurance steps in for emergency evacuations, ensuring prompt medical attention or a safe return to your home country.

5. COVID-19 Assurance:
   - Given the ongoing global situation, travel insurance with COVID-19 coverage is indispensable. It shields against virus-related unexpected situations, covering medical expenses and trip interruptions.

Health Preparation Tips:

1. Connect with Your Healthcare Provider:
   - Before your journey, consult with your healthcare provider. Discuss travel plans, and pre-existing health conditions, and get necessary vaccinations or medications.

2. Pack Essential Medications:
    - Carry an ample supply of prescribed medications. Include a basic first aid kit with essentials like pain relievers, antihistamines, and medications recommended by your healthcare provider.

3. Stay Informed:
    - Keep an eye on travel advisories and health alerts for the region. Check your government's travel department website for the latest information and recommendations.

4. Hydrate and Eat Well:
    - Maintain good health by staying hydrated, especially during outdoor activities. Prioritize a balanced diet with fresh fruits and vegetables to support your immune system.

5. Travel Safely:
    - Practice good hygiene with frequent handwashing and hand sanitizer use. Follow local standards to ensure a safe voyage.

6. Emergency Preparedness:
    - Keep a list of emergency contacts and your healthcare provider's details. Carry

necessary health documentation, including insurance details and a list of allergies or medical conditions.

Packing Tips and Essentials

Packing for a Devon adventure demands thoughtful planning due to its diverse landscapes and ever-changing weather. Whether you're exploring coastal paths, visiting historic sites, or lounging on the beaches, this comprehensive packing guide guarantees a comfortable and enjoyable stay in Devon.

Clothing Essentials

1. Layers for Unpredictable Weather:
    - Devon's weather can shift unexpectedly. Pack lightweight, breathable clothing for easy layering, allowing you to adapt to temperature changes. A waterproof jacket is essential for sudden rain, and comfortable walking shoes are a necessity for urban and nature exploration.

2. Swimwear for Beach Activities:
    - If you're hitting the beaches or indulging in water activities, bring swimwear for a refreshing sea dip or water sports.

3. Warm Layers for Cool Evenings:
    - Evenings can be chilly. Pack a sweater or light jacket to stay cozy during sunset walks or outdoor dinners.

Outdoor Gear

4. Compact Daypack:
    - A comfortable, compact backpack is essential for day trips, hikes, and carrying essentials. Ensure it has enough space for water, snacks, and any treasures you collect.

5. Walking Poles for Stability:
    - Explore Devon's varied landscapes with stability using walking poles, especially beneficial in areas like Dartmoor National Park.

6. Binoculars for Wildlife Watching:
    - Capture the beauty of Devon's landscapes and wildlife with binoculars, perfect for bird watching along the coast or in nature reserves.

7. Reusable Water Bottle:
    - Stay hydrated during outdoor activities and minimize environmental impact with a reusable water bottle.

Electronics

8. Camera/Smartphone for Memories:
    - Capture Devon's beauty and history. Don't forget chargers and extra memory cards to ensure you capture every photo-worthy moment.

9. Power Bank for Uninterrupted Exploration:
    - Keep your devices charged, especially during long days of exploration. A power bank ensures you stay connected even when outlets are scarce.

Devon's charm lies in its diverse experiences, and with this packing guide, you're equipped for every adventure the region has to offer. Enjoy your trip!

CHAPTER 3
EXPLORING THE REGIONS

Regions of Devon

Discover the captivating diversity of Devon, a charming county in southwest England celebrated for its varied landscapes and picturesque settings. Here's a glimpse into the distinct regions that define Devon's allure:

1. North Devon:
Explore North Devon's rugged coastline, sandy beaches, and market towns, a paradise for surfers. Inland, rolling hills and charming villages enhance the scenic beauty.

Highlights: Exmoor National Park, Ilfracombe, Barnstaple, Braunton Burrows.

2. East Devon:
Marvel at East Devon's stunning Jurassic Coast, a UNESCO World Heritage Site with fossil-rich cliffs. Coastal towns, villages, and lush countryside abound, featuring the East Devon Area of Outstanding Natural Beauty (AONB).

Highlights: Sidmouth, Exmouth, Jurassic Coast, East Devon AONB.

3. South Devon:
South Devon beckons with estuaries, sandy coves, and rolling hills, offering a mild climate and a playground for water-based activities. Quaint towns and historic sites add to the region's allure.

Highlights: Dartmouth, Salcombe, Torquay, Dartmoor National Park.

4. West Devon:
Immerse yourself in West Devon's rural landscapes, ancient woodlands, and Dartmoor National Park's untamed beauty. Tranquil escapes await, complemented by historical sites, market towns, and outdoor adventures.

Highlights: Tavistock, Okehampton, Dartmoor National Park, Lydford Gorge.

5. Mid Devon:
Nestled between Exmoor and Dartmoor, Mid Devon offers a blend of countryside and market towns. The Grand Western Canal weaves through, providing scenic walks and boat trips, showcasing the region's agricultural heritage and traditional charm.

Highlights: Tiverton, Crediton, Grand Western Canal.

Must-See Attractions

Discover the enchanting wonders of Devon, a captivating county in southwest England, where history, nature, and culture converge to create a tapestry of unforgettable experiences. Whether you're a nature enthusiast, a history buff, or simply seeking tranquility, Devon has something special for everyone. Here's a guide to the must-see attractions that should grace every traveler's itinerary:

1. Dartmoor National Park
Immerse yourself in the untamed beauty of Dartmoor, a vast landscape adorned with granite tors, ancient ruins, and meandering rivers. Haytor,

an iconic tor, offers panoramic views. Explore diverse ecosystems, hike scenic trails, and encounter Dartmoor ponies freely roaming.

2. Jurassic Coast
Unearth the geological marvels along the Devon coastline at the UNESCO World Heritage Site, the Jurassic Coast. From the iconic Durdle Door to the fossil-rich Lyme Regis, the coastal landscapes and charming Lulworth Cove reveal Earth's history etched in stone.

3. Exeter Cathedral
Step into the rich religious heritage of Devon at Exeter Cathedral, a Gothic masterpiece dating back to the 11th century. Marvel at stunning stained glass, and intricate carvings, and explore the tranquil cloister. Guided tours offer insights into the cathedral's history.

4. RHS Garden Rosemoor
Find serenity amidst vibrant blooms at RHS Garden Rosemoor. Explore themed gardens, attend seasonal events, and appreciate the diverse collection of plants in this horticultural haven.

5. Clovelly
Transport yourself to the past in the picturesque fishing village of Clovelly. Cobbled streets,

traditional cottages, and a traffic-free environment create an enchanting atmosphere. Explore the historic harbor and embrace the timeless beauty of this coastal gem.

6. Plymouth Hoe and the Royal Citadel
Plymouth Hoe's waterfront, with Smeaton's Tower lighthouse, offers stunning views of Plymouth Sound. Explore the historic Royal Citadel, a 17th-century fortress guarding Plymouth's harbor entrance.

Off-the-Beaten-Path Destinations

While popular attractions draw crowds, Devon holds hidden gems for those seeking a more intimate experience. Explore these lesser-known destinations:

1. Finch Foundry
Uncover Devon's industrial past at Finch Foundry in Sticklepath. Operated by the National Trust, this water-powered forge showcases blacksmithing traditions.

2. A La Ronde
Near Exmouth, A La Ronde is an extraordinary 18th-century house with a unique sixteen-sided

design. Wander through quirky rooms adorned with shells and feathers, surrounded by enchanting gardens.

3. Valley of the Rocks

Escape to the tranquility of the Valley of the Rocks near Lynton. Towering cliffs, rugged rock formations, and panoramic views make it a haven for hikers and nature enthusiasts.

4. Coleton Fish Acre

Embrace the elegance of Coleton Fishacre, a hidden Arts and Crafts gem near Dartmouth. Explore the 1920s country home and its lush gardens overlooking the sea.

5. Burgh Island

Accessible by sea tractor, Burgh Island off the South Devon coast exudes glamor. Explore the Art Deco Burgh Island Hotel, walk sandy beaches, and soak in the unique atmosphere.

6. Fingle Bridge

Tucked in Dartmoor National Park, Fingle Bridge offers a peaceful retreat. Cross the ancient stone bridge, enjoy riverside walks, and savor refreshments at the nearby Fingle Bridge Inn.

CHAPTER 4
ACCOMMODATIONS OPTIONS

Hotels and Resorts in Devon

Devon, blessed with captivating landscapes and a rich cultural heritage, presents an enticing array of hotels and resorts tailored to diverse preferences. Whether you're yearning for seaside luxury or the tranquility of the countryside, Devon's accommodation options promise to elevate your travel experience.

1. Salcombe Harbour Hotel (Salcombe)
Nestled on the shores of Salcombe Estuary, the Salcombe Harbour Hotel is a beacon of seaside luxury. With its contemporary design and stunning coastal views, it promises an unforgettable escape in one of Devon's most scenic locations.

Amenities:
1. Spa and Wellness Center: Indulge in the on-site spa offering a range of treatments and therapies, complemented by serene estuary views.
2. Harbour-View Suites: The hotel's suites provide panoramic views of the estuary, ensuring a truly immersive coastal experience.
3. Culinary Excellence: Guests can enjoy exquisite dining at the hotel's restaurant, where locally sourced ingredients are crafted into culinary masterpieces.
4. Outdoor Terrace: Relax on the outdoor terrace overlooking the estuary, perfect for enjoying a leisurely afternoon tea or cocktails at sunset.
5. Water Sports Access: For the adventurous, the hotel offers easy access to water sports, allowing guests to explore the estuary from a different perspective.

Overall Impression:
The Salcombe Harbour Hotel combines modern luxury with coastal charm, creating an idyllic retreat for those seeking a sophisticated seaside experience.

2. Paschoe House (Crediton)

Situated near the market town of Crediton, Paschoe House is a country retreat that seamlessly blends historic elegance with contemporary comforts. Surrounded by acres of lush countryside, it offers a tranquil escape in the heart of Devon.

Amenities:
1. Country House Ambiance: Guests can immerse themselves in the grandeur of a restored country house with individually designed rooms reflecting a perfect blend of history and modernity.
2. Dining Excellence: The hotel's restaurant serves gastronomic delights using locally sourced produce, creating a farm-to-fork dining experience.
3. Picturesque Gardens: Explore the beautifully landscaped gardens, providing a serene setting for a leisurely stroll or afternoon tea.
4. Private Events and Weddings: With its elegant spaces, Paschoe House is an ideal venue for private events and weddings, offering bespoke services for special occasions.

5. Cookery School: For those passionate about culinary arts, the hotel offers cookery classes where guests can learn from skilled chefs in a hands-on environment.

Overall Impression:
Pascoe House is a testament to refined country living, offering guests a chance to unwind in a historic setting surrounded by the natural beauty of Devon's countryside.

3. Bovey Castle (Dartmoor National Park)
Nestled within Dartmoor National Park, Bovey Castle stands as a luxurious retreat set against the backdrop of captivating landscapes. This grand estate seamlessly marries historic charm with modern opulence, creating an unrivaled Devonshire experience.

Amenities:
1. Championship Golf Course: Golf enthusiasts can indulge in a round of golf on the hotel's 18-hole championship course, surrounded by the breathtaking scenery of Dartmoor.
2. Elegant Country Rooms: Bovey Castle's rooms exude sophistication, offering plush furnishings and panoramic views of the estate grounds.

3. Falconry Experiences: Guests can partake in unique falconry experiences, getting up close and personal with majestic birds of prey under the guidance of expert falconers.
4. Fine Dining at Great Western Restaurant: The Great Western Restaurant offers an exquisite dining experience, showcasing the finest local produce in an opulent setting.
5. Outdoor Activities: From archery to fishing, Bovey Castle provides a range of outdoor activities, allowing guests to immerse themselves in the natural beauty of Dartmoor.

Overall Impression:
Bovey Castle is a haven of refined country living, providing guests with an opulent escape amidst the idyllic landscapes of Dartmoor. With an array of amenities catering to both leisure and adventure, this hotel promises an unforgettable stay for those seeking the epitome of countryside elegance.

4. The Victoria Hotel (Sidmouth)
Perched on the East Devon coast in Sidmouth, The Victoria Hotel is a classic seaside retreat offering timeless charm and modern comforts. Overlooking Lyme Bay provides an elegant haven for those seeking a quintessential coastal experience.

Amenities:
1. Sea View Rooms: Guests can wake up to breathtaking views of the sea from the comfort of their well-appointed rooms, creating a serene and relaxing atmosphere.
2. Lounge and Terrace: The hotel's lounge and terrace provide the perfect spots to unwind with a book or enjoy afternoon tea while taking in panoramic views of the Jurassic Coast.
3. Indoor and Outdoor Pools: For relaxation, guests can choose between the indoor and outdoor pools, both surrounded by lush gardens and offering a tranquil setting.
4. Fine Dining at The Jubilee Restaurant: Indulge in culinary delights at The Jubilee Restaurant, where an extensive menu features locally sourced ingredients and a selection of fine wines.
5. Coastal Walks and Activities: The Victoria Hotel offers easy access to scenic coastal walks and a variety of activities, allowing guests to explore the beauty of the Jurassic Coast.

Overall Impression:
The Victoria Hotel combines Victorian elegance with coastal tranquility, offering guests a timeless experience along the stunning East Devon coastline.

5. The Barnstaple Hotel (Barnstaple)

Situated in the heart of North Devon, The Barnstaple Hotel provides a modern and comfortable stay with easy access to the region's attractions. This contemporary hotel offers a blend of convenience and leisure in a bustling market town.

Amenities:
1. Modernist Accommodations: The hotel features well-appointed rooms with modern amenities, providing a comfortable retreat for both business and leisure travelers.
2. Leisure Facilities: Guests can enjoy the hotel's leisure facilities, including an indoor heated pool, fitness center, and spa treatments, providing relaxation after a day of exploration.
3. Family-Friendly Atmosphere: With family rooms and a welcoming ambiance, The Barnstaple Hotel is suitable for travelers with children, offering a convenient base for family adventures.
4. Dining at The Brasserie: The hotel's Brasserie restaurant serves a diverse menu, from hearty breakfasts to evening meals,

offering a range of options to suit various tastes.
5. Conference and Event Spaces: For business travelers, The Barnstaple Hotel provides conference and event spaces, making it an ideal venue for meetings, conferences, and special occasions.

Overall Impression:
The Barnstaple Hotel offers a contemporary and convenient stay in North Devon, catering to a diverse range of travelers with its modern amenities and family-friendly atmosphere.

Charming Bed and Breakfast

For those craving a personal touch and an intimate experience, Devon's bed and breakfasts (B&Bs) offer a warm and welcoming retreat. These charming accommodations provide a taste of local life, ensuring a home away from home.

1. Coastal Charms

Seabreeze Bed & Breakfast (Plymouth):
Overlooking Plymouth Sound, Seabreeze combines modern comforts with a welcoming atmosphere. Enjoy breathtaking views while immersing yourself in the heart of Plymouth.

Belmont Bed and Breakfast (Sidmouth):
Nestled in Sidmouth, Belmont offers seafront elegance and easy access to town attractions. Experience the charm of Devon's coast in a cozy and inviting setting.

2. Countryside Retreats:

The Old Parsonage (Dartmoor):
Escape to tranquility at The Old Parsonage in Dartmoor. This historic B&B boasts beautifully decorated rooms, providing a peaceful retreat in the heart of the countryside.

The Old Dairy at Bishops Barton (Exmoor):
On a working farm near Exmoor, The Old Dairy offers a serene countryside escape. Experience rural charm while enjoying modern amenities in this delightful B&B.

3. Historic Elegance:

Gages Mill Country Guest House (Dartmoor):
Set in a former 17th-century mill near Dartmoor, Gages Mill seamlessly blends historic features with modern comforts. Immerse yourself in Devon's rich heritage at this elegant guest house.

The Court Barn (Holsworthy):
A 16th-century thatched cottage, The Court Barn in Holsworthy provides an authentic taste of Devon's heritage. Experience the charm of centuries past in this cozy and historic B&B.

4. Family-Friendly Comfort:

Rowcroft Lodge (Paignton):
Ideal for families, Rowcroft Lodge in Paignton offers spacious family rooms and a friendly atmosphere. It serves as a perfect base for exploring nearby attractions, including Paignton Zoo.

Mariners Guesthouse (Plymouth):
Situated in Plymouth, Mariners Guesthouse provides a welcoming environment for families. With comfortable rooms and proximity to the city's waterfront, it ensures a delightful family-friendly stay.

5. Romantic Getaways:

The Old Vicarage (Otterton):
For a romantic weekend, The Old Vicarage in Otterton offers individually styled rooms amidst

picturesque landscapes. Experience the charm of this romantic retreat in Devon.

Barton Cross Hotel (Exeter):
Nestled in Exeter, Barton Cross Hotel's beautiful gardens and intimate setting make it an ideal choice for a romantic escape close to the city. Enjoy a romantic getaway surrounded by Devon's natural beauty.

Camping and RV Options in Devon

For nature enthusiasts and those seeking a more outdoorsy experience, Devon's camping and RV parks offer a chance to immerse oneself in the county's natural beauty. From coastal campsites to idyllic spots in the heart of the countryside, Devon provides a diverse range of camping options.

1. Coastal Camping Bliss: Ladram Bay Holiday Park (Near Sidmouth)
Charm:
Experience coastal camping bliss at Ladram Bay Holiday Park, nestled near Sidmouth. Revel in stunning sea views from spacious pitches, some overlooking the sea, creating a serene setting for outdoor enthusiasts.

Benefits:

1. Seafront Access: Direct access to the beach for seaside strolls, water activities, and breathtaking sunsets.
2. Family-Friendly Facilities: Catering to families with pools, entertainment options, and diverse amenities for all ages.
3. Scenic Coastal Walks: Explore the South West Coast Path for picturesque walks along the Jurassic Coast.

2. Riverside Retreats: Exe Valley Campsite (Near Tiverton)

Charm:

Find tranquility at Exe Valley Campsite near Tiverton, offering a riverside retreat along the River Exe. Immerse yourself in a peaceful escape, surrounded by the natural beauty of the river.

Benefits:
1. Riverside Pitches: Camp close to the calming sounds of the River Exe, creating a soothing atmosphere.
2. Nature Immersion: Enjoy riverside walks, birdwatching, and a chance to disconnect from the hustle and bustle.
3. Campfire Friendly: Traditional camping experience with designated areas for campfires, enhancing the outdoor ambiance.

3. Dartmoor Wilderness: Langstone Manor (Near Tavistock)

Charm:

Langstone Manor near Tavistock offers a camping experience immersed in Dartmoor's rugged beauty. With moorland surroundings, this campsite provides a true escape into nature.

Benefits:
1. Dartmoor Access: Direct access to Dartmoor National Park, with walking and hiking trails leading from the campsite.
2. Starry Nights: Experience the enchanting Dartmoor night sky with minimal light pollution, ideal for stargazing.
3. Tranquil Setting: Camp in a peaceful environment, with spacious pitches allowing for a sense of seclusion.

4. Family-Friendly Campgrounds: Cofton Holidays (Near Dawlish)

Charm:

Cofton Holidays near Dawlish caters to families, offering a fun and comfortable camping experience. The site provides family-friendly facilities and activities for a memorable outdoor getaway.

Benefits:
1. Indoor and Outdoor Fun: Indoor pool, playgrounds, and entertainment options for the whole family.
2. Easy Beach Access: Near Dawlish Warren, providing easy access to the beach for sandcastle building and seaside adventures.
3. Pet-Friendly Facilities: Welcoming furry family members, making it an excellent choice for pet-loving outdoor enthusiasts.

5. RV Parks with Scenic Views: Riverside Caravan & Camping Park (South Molton)

Charm:

Riverside Caravan & Camping Park in South Molton caters to RV enthusiasts, offering a scenic setting along the River Mole. Surrounded by countryside views, it provides a delightful retreat for motorhome travelers.

Benefits:
1. Spacious RV Pitches: Ample space for RVs, ensuring a comfortable and scenic base for exploration.
2. Riverside Relaxation: Enjoy the calming presence of the River Mole, with

opportunities for riverside walks and relaxation.
3. Countryside Exploration: Ideal starting point for exploring Exmoor National Park and North Devon's countryside.

Vacation Rentals in Devon

For those seeking independence and a more immersive experience, vacation rentals in Devon provide a homey atmosphere with the flexibility to explore the region at your own pace. From cottages in the countryside to apartments by the sea, Devon's vacation rentals cater to a variety of preferences.

1. Coastal Cottages:

The Beach House (Croyde):
Direct beach access and a cozy retreat await at The Beach House in Croyde. Perfect for surf enthusiasts, it offers stunning sea views and a comfortable haven after a day of seaside adventures.

Sea View Cottage (Beer):
For a traditional seaside experience with modern comforts, Sea View Cottage in Beer is an ideal choice. Enjoy the charm of this coastal village and relax with panoramic sea views.

2. Countryside Retreats:

The Linhay (Near Totnes):
Escape to tranquility with The Linhay near Totnes. Surrounded by rolling hills and farmland, this vacation rental provides a peaceful retreat while keeping you close to the attractions of South Devon.

3. Historic Homes:
Coach House at Buckland Abbey (Near Yelverton): Experience the charm of historic living at the Coach House at Buckland Abbey. This beautifully restored coach house near Yelverton offers a unique blend of history and comfort.

4. Family-Friendly Accommodations:

Flear Farm Cottages (Near Dartmouth):
Ideal for families, Flear Farm Cottages near Dartmouth provide a spacious and comfortable base. On-site amenities, including a swimming pool and play areas, ensure an enjoyable stay for all.

5. Urban Apartments:

The Quay Exeter:

Explore Devon's cities while enjoying the comforts of home at The Quay Exeter. Located on Exeter's historic quayside, it offers modern apartments with easy access to the city's attractions.

Hostels and Budget Accommodations

For budget-conscious travelers, Devon's hostels and budget accommodations provide an affordable yet comfortable base for exploration. These options cater to various needs, from solo backpackers to groups of friends looking for cost-effective stays.

1. Globe Backpackers (Exeter)

Charm:
Explore Exeter on a budget at Globe Backpackers, centrally located with a vibrant and social atmosphere. Embrace the camaraderie in affordable dormitory-style rooms, perfect for solo travelers and groups.

Benefits:
1. Affordable Dorms: Budget-friendly dormitory accommodation fostering a sense of community.

2. Central Location: Explore Exeter's attractions, shops, and transport easily from the heart of the city.
3. Social Events: Engage with fellow travelers through organized social events.

2. Ilfracombe Backpackers (Ilfracombe)

Charm:
Experience laid-back charm at Ilfracombe Backpackers, a budget-friendly option in the coastal town of Ilfracombe. Enjoy a relaxed atmosphere and proximity to North Devon's coastal beauty.

Benefits:
- Budget-Friendly Rates: Affordable rates without compromising essential amenities.
- Coastal Proximity: Explore North Devon's coastline and indulge in seaside activities.
- Community Vibes: Shared facilities fostering a sense of community among budget-conscious travelers.

3. The Exeter YHA (Dartmoor National Park)

Charm:
Immerse yourself in Dartmoor's natural beauty on a budget at the Exeter YHA, nestled in Dartmoor

National Park. A cost-effective base for exploring the park's trails and landscapes.

Benefits:
1. Dartmoor Access: An affordable stay within Dartmoor, perfect for exploring the park.
2. Group-Friendly: Catering to both solo travelers and groups with dormitories and private rooms.
3. Educational Programs: Enrich your travel experience with educational programs about Dartmoor's flora, fauna, and history.

4. YHA Dartmouth (Dartmouth)

Charm:
Combine affordability with a scenic location at YHA Dartmouth in the picturesque town of Dartmouth. Overlooking the River Dart, this hostel offers budget travelers a welcoming place to stay.

Benefits:
1. Riverside Setting: Enjoy beautiful views and a peaceful ambiance by the riverside.
2. AffordableAccommodation: Budget-friendly options, including shared dormitories and private rooms.

3. Dartmouth Exploration: Easy access to Dartmouth's attractions without breaking the bank.

5. The Quarryman's Rest (Bampton)

Charm:
Discover affordable accommodations in the countryside near Bampton at The Quarryman's Rest. Embrace the tranquility of village life in a cozy and budget-friendly setting.

Benefits:
1. Village Retreat: Experience the serenity of village life while staying within budget.
2. Affordable Rooms: Budget-conscious accommodation for travelers exploring the Devon countryside.
3. Local Pub Atmosphere: Associated with a local pub, providing an authentic village culture experience.

CHAPTER 5
FOOD AND DINING

Devon's Culinary Tapestry

Nestled in the captivating landscapes of the South West, Devon's culinary scene is a delightful tapestry of flavors that reflects the county's diverse influences and rich agricultural heritage. From the coastal abundance of the English Channel to the fertile farmlands of the countryside, Devon cuisine is a celebration of fresh, locally sourced ingredients and a testament to the region's culinary prowess.

Coastal Abundance: Seafood Extravaganza

Influences:
Devon's extensive coastline, stretching along the English Channel, infuses its cuisine with an abundance of seafood. The vibrant fishing ports, such as Brixham, Teignmouth, and Salcombe, play a pivotal role in bringing the daily catch to the tables of local establishments.

Flavors:
Indulge in the briny goodness of succulent scallops, the delicate sweetness of crab, and the robust flavors of mackerel. The "Catch of the Day"

concept in seaside towns like Brixham ensures that the seafood served is not only fresh but also a testament to the maritime heritage of the region.

Fertile Countryside: Hearty and Satisfying

Influences:
The verdant countryside of Devon contributes to hearty and satisfying dishes, with a focus on seasonal produce and locally reared livestock. The fertile soil allows for the cultivation of a variety of crops, influencing the county's farm-to-table ethos.

Flavors:
Savor the earthy goodness of root vegetables, the sweetness of freshly picked berries, and the robust flavors of locally raised meats. The Devonshire Pasty, with its flaky pastry and savory filling of meat and vegetables, encapsulates the essence of the county's countryside cuisine.

Dairy Excellence: Creamy Indulgence

Influences:
Devon is renowned for its dairy excellence, with lush pastures providing ideal conditions for dairy farming. The county's dairy products, including cream, cheese, and butter, have earned a reputation for their rich and creamy textures.

Flavors:

Indulge in the velvety richness of Devon Cream, a luxurious addition to desserts and teas. The artisanal cheeses, such as the distinctively flavored Vulscombe Goat Cheese, showcase the county's commitment to preserving and celebrating its dairy heritage.

Orchard Bliss: Cider Culture

Influences:

Devon's apple orchards contribute to the creation of exceptional cider, making the county a hub for cider culture. The craft of cider-making has been passed down through generations, resulting in a diverse range of flavors and styles.

Flavors:

Sip on the sweet notes of traditional farmhouse cider or savor the complexity of craft brews. Devon's cider offerings provide a refreshing and quintessentially English experience, with orchards often opening their doors for tours and tastings.

Farmers' Markets: A Showcase of Local Bounty

Influences:
Devon's vibrant farmers' markets are a testament to the county's commitment to showcasing local bounty. Farmers, artisans, and producers gather to offer a diverse array of products, from fresh produce to handmade cheeses and preserves.

Flavors:
Explore the seasonal delights of the markets, sampling ripe fruits, artisanal bread, and locally crafted delicacies. The markets not only provide an opportunity to taste the flavors of Devon but also connect visitors with the passionate producers behind the county's culinary treasures.

Fusion of Influences: International Culinary Diversity

Influences:
Devon's culinary scene is not bound by traditional English flavors alone. The country's cosmopolitan towns and cities welcome influences from around the world, creating a diverse and international dining landscape.

Flavors:

Explore the eclectic menus of Devon's restaurants, where flavors from Asia, the Mediterranean, and beyond meld seamlessly with local ingredients. From fusion cuisine to international twists on traditional dishes, the culinary diversity in Devon adds a dynamic dimension to the gastronomic experience.

Popular Dishes and Local Specialties

Embark on a gastronomic journey through Devon, where each bite is a celebration of the region's rich flavors and culinary heritage. Here's a mouthwatering list of popular dishes and local specialties that are a must-try for an authentic Devonshire culinary experience:

1. Cream Tea
Indulge in a classic Cream Tea at The Singing Kettle in Dartmouth or The Vintage Tea House in Exeter. Enjoy freshly baked scones accompanied by clotted cream and strawberry jam, paired with a cup of locally sourced tea.

2. Fisherman's Pie
Savor the coastal comfort of Fisherman's Pie at The Seahorse in Dartmouth or Rockfish in Plymouth. This savory dish features a medley of locally caught

fish topped with creamy mashed potatoes, capturing the essence of Devon's maritime influences.

3. Devonshire Pasty
Try an authentic Devonshire Pasty at Chunk of Devon in Ottery St Mary. This handheld delight is filled with a savory mix of locally sourced meat, vegetables, and potatoes, making it a perfect on-the-go snack for countryside exploration.

4. Devonshire Honey
Discover the sweetness of Devonshire Honey at Tavistock Farmers' Market. Local beekeepers showcase their golden elixir with varied floral notes, providing a taste of Devon's thriving beekeeping heritage.

5. Devon Cider
Sip on liquid gold at Sandford Orchards or Ashridge Cider. Experience the diverse flavors of Devon's cider culture, from sweet farmhouse blends to complex craft brews, in the heart of the county's picturesque orchards.

6. Eccles Cake
End your culinary journey with an Eccles Cake at the Real Food Store in Exeter. This sweet treat, though not native to Devon, adds a delightful touch

to your dessert experience with its flaky pastry and spiced currant filling.

7. Devon Blue Cheese
Delight in the creamy excellence of Devon Blue Cheese at Country Cheeses in Tavistock. This locally produced artisanal cheese offers a unique flavor profile and is a perfect addition to any cheese lover's palate.

Best Restaurants and Dining Experiences

Devon's culinary scene offers a diverse array of dining experiences, from top-rated establishments to hidden gems that capture the essence of global cuisines. Whether you're seeking refined gastronomy or exploring local treasures, here's a curated list that showcases the richness and diversity of Devon's restaurant landscape:

1. The Elephant, Torquay (Modern British)
Type: Michelin-starred
Situated in Torquay, The Elephant is a culinary gem that showcases modern British cuisine. With a Michelin-starred chef at the helm, the restaurant offers a refined dining experience with a focus on locally sourced ingredients. The panoramic views of

Torbay add to the ambiance, making it a top-rated destination for culinary enthusiasts.

2. River Exe Café, Exmouth (Seafood)
Type: Floating Restaurant
For a unique seafood experience, head to the River Exe Café in Exmouth. Accessible only by boat, this floating restaurant allows diners to enjoy fresh catches while surrounded by the tranquil waters of the Exe Estuary. It's a hidden gem that combines the beauty of the sea with a diverse seafood menu.

3. The Maltsters Arms, Tuckenhay (Traditional Pub Fare)
Type: Riverside Pub
Nestled along the Dart River in Tuckenhay, The Maltsters Arms is a traditional pub that combines riverside charm with exceptional dining. Serving hearty dishes crafted with local ingredients, this hidden gem offers a welcoming atmosphere, making it a favorite among locals and savvy visitors.

4.Gidleigh Park, Chagford (Gastronomic Elegance)
Type: Michelin-starred Country House Hotel
For an unparalleled gastronomic experience, visit Gidleigh Park in Chagford. With two Michelin stars, this country house hotel and restaurant offer refined menus crafted by renowned chefs. The

historic and luxurious surroundings add to the overall elegance of this top-rated establishment.

5. The Crab Shed, Salcombe (Seafood)
Type: Seaside Restaurant
Situated in the picturesque town of Salcombe, The Crab Shed celebrates the region's maritime influences with a focus on fresh seafood. Overlooking the estuary, this seaside restaurant offers a casual and laid-back atmosphere, allowing diners to savor the flavors of the sea while enjoying stunning coastal views.

6. The Nobody Inn, Doddiscombsleigh (Gastro Pub)
Type: Gastropub
The Nobody Inn in Doddiscombsleigh offers a charming gastropub experience, showcasing a menu crafted with locally sourced ingredients. The Devonshire Burger, made with the finest beef and accompanied by fresh, seasonal toppings, is a highlight that reflects the establishment's commitment to quality.

Dietary Preferences and Restrictions

Devon, nestled in the heart of the South West, is a culinary haven that not only respects but celebrates diverse dietary preferences. Whether you're a vegetarian, vegan, or have gluten sensitivities,

Devon's rich and varied food scene offers a delectable array of options.

1. Vegetarian Bliss

Devon warmly welcomes vegetarians with a spectrum of flavorful choices highlighting locally sourced vegetables. Check out these notable establishments:

The Real Food Store, Exeter:
Indulge in a varied menu featuring nutrient-packed salads, savory wraps, and sandwiches. The casual and vibrant ambiance makes it an ideal spot for a wholesome vegetarian meal.

The Maltsters Arms, Tuckenhay:
This riverside pub offers creatively crafted vegetarian options, showcasing seasonal produce amidst a traditional pub atmosphere with scenic views of the Dart River.

2. Embracing Vegan Delights

For those embracing a vegan lifestyle, Devon boasts a delightful array of plant-based options with a focus on fresh, cruelty-free ingredients:

Real Food Store, Exeter:
Discover creative salads, plant-based wraps, and hearty vegan bowls in a modern and vibrant setting.

Don't forget to explore the sweet conclusion with vegan desserts and snacks.

The Orange Tree, Torquay:
Enjoy a stylish environment at The Orange Tree, featuring a diverse menu with a dedicated section for delectable vegan dishes, complementing its innovative plant-based offerings.

3. Gluten-Free Treats
Devon understands the significance of catering to gluten-free dietary needs, ensuring those with sensitivities can relish mouthwatering meals:

The Cadeleigh Arms, near Tiverton:
A haven for gluten-free diners, The Cadeleigh Arms provides a dedicated menu featuring a variety of dishes crafted with gluten-free ingredients in a welcoming traditional pub setting.

The Rock Inn, Haytor Vale:
Committed to providing allergen-friendly menus, The Rock Inn offers a safe and enjoyable dining experience for those with specific dietary requirements. Guests can savor gluten-free options in the charming ambiance of the Devonshire countryside.

CHAPTER 6
TOURS AND ATTRACTIONS

Guided Tours and Excursions

Discover the diverse landscapes and rich history of Devon through a selection of curated guided tours and excursions. Whether you crave coastal adventures, historical revelations, or nature immersion, these experiences promise a unique exploration of the region.

Coastal Marvels

Coastal Explorer: Sea Kayaking Expedition
 Embark on a unique sea kayaking expedition along Devon's captivating coastline with Coastal Explorer. Paddle by rugged cliffs, explore hidden sea caves,

and witness marine life up close. This guided tour caters to adventurers of all skill levels.

Highlights:
1. Expert-guided exploration of sea caves and rock formations.
2. Chance encounters with seals, dolphins, and coastal birdlife.
3. Equipment and instruction provided for all experience levels.

Tour Operator: Coastal Explorer

Jurassic Coast Safari: Fossil Hunting Expedition
Join a guided fossil hunting expedition along the UNESCO World Heritage Site, the Jurassic Coast. Led by expert guides, this hands-on excursion allows participants to discover ancient fossils embedded in the cliffs.

Highlights:
1. Visit fossil-rich locations along the Jurassic Coast.
2. Understand the geology and history of the place.
3. Hands-on fossil hunting with expert guidance.

Tour Operator: Jurassic Coast Guides

Dartmoor Discoveries: Guided Walking Tour

Immerse yourself in the untamed beauty of Dartmoor National Park with a guided walking tour by Dartmoor Tours. Trained guides lead participants through ancient woodlands, open moorland, and historical sites, offering insights into the park's unique flora, fauna, and folklore.

Highlights:
1. Scenic walks to ancient stone circles and tors.
2. Interpretation of Dartmoor's rich history and myths.
3. Encounters with Dartmoor's iconic ponies and wildlife.

Tour Operator: Dartmoor Tours

River Exe Wildlife Cruise

Embark on a serene wildlife cruise along the River Exe with Stuart Line Cruises. This guided excursion offers the opportunity to spot seals, seabirds, and other wildlife against the picturesque backdrop of the Exe Estuary.

Highlights:

- Scenic cruise past Powderham Castle and Topsham.
- Expert commentary on the river's ecology and wildlife.
- Binoculars provided for optimal wildlife viewing.

Tour Operator: Stuart Line Cruises

Historical Revelations

Exeter Cathedral Guided Tour

Delve into centuries of history with a guided tour of Exeter Cathedral. Led by knowledgeable guides, explore the stunning architecture, medieval artifacts, and hidden gems within the cathedral's walls.

Highlights:
1. Detailed examination of intricate stained glass windows.
2. Access to the cathedral library's rare book collection.
3. Stories of the cathedral's role in Exeter's history.

Tour Operator: Exeter Cathedral Tours

Totnes Time Travel: Historic Walking Tour

Embark on a journey through time with the Totnes Time Travel guided walking tour. Led by costumed guides, this theatrical experience takes participants through Totnes' historic streets, sharing tales of kings, rebels, and intriguing characters from the past.

Highlights:
1. Interactive storytelling by costumed guides.
2. Visit historic sites, including Totnes Castle.
3. Engaging narratives of Totnes' colorful history.

Tour Operator: Totnes Time Travel

Cultural Exploration

Dartmoor Prison Museum Tour

Gain insight into the history of Dartmoor Prison with a guided tour of the Dartmoor Prison Museum. Explore the prison's evolution, view historical artifacts, and learn about the lives of both staff and inmates through engaging exhibits.

Highlights:

1. Visit the museum's collection of prison memorabilia.
2. Understand the impact of Dartmoor Prison on the local community.
3. Guided tour with informative commentary.

Tour Operator: Dartmoor Prison Museum

Devon Distillery Tour: Craft Gin and Whiskey Experience
Indulge in a unique cultural experience with a guided tour of a Devon distillery. Discover the art of crafting gin and whiskey, from the selection of botanicals to the distillation process. Tastings and insights into the distillery's history add to the experience.

Highlights:
1. Behind-the-scenes tour of the distillation process.
2. Tasting sessions with locally created spirits.
3. Knowledgeable guides sharing the art of distilling.

Historic Sites and Landmarks

Delve into Devon's millennia-old history with a journey through its iconic landmarks and cultural sites. Each site holds a unique significance, offering a glimpse into the rich tapestry of the county's past.

1. Exeter Cathedral - Exeter

Exeter Cathedral, also known as the Cathedral Church of Saint Peter, stands as a Gothic masterpiece in the heart of Exeter for over 900 years. Its construction commenced in 1114, witnessing centuries of historical events.

Cultural Significance:
1. Marvel at stunning vaulted ceilings, medieval stained glass, and intricate carvings.
2. The cathedral has been a focal point for religious worship and civic events throughout Exeter's history.
3. Explore the Exeter Cathedral Library, housing rare and ancient manuscripts.

2. Powderham Castle - Kenton

Dating back to the 14th century, Powderham Castle, a fortified manor, graces the banks of the River Exe. Overlooking the estuary, it has witnessed centuries of political and social changes.

Cultural Significance:
1. Discover historical interiors, including the Victorian kitchen and the breathtaking music room.
2. Explore the grounds with gardens designed by Capability Brown.
3. For for than 600 years, the Courtenay family has called this place home.

3. Buckland Abbey - Yelverton

Originally a 13th-century Cistercian monastery, Buckland Abbey transformed into the residence of Sir Francis Drake in the 16th century.

Cultural Significance:
1. Walk in the footsteps of Sir Francis Drake and explore his former residence.
2. Admire the Great Barn, a testament to medieval architecture.
3. The abbey houses a collection of Drake memorabilia and artifacts.

4. Tavistock Abbey - Tavistock

Founded in the 10th century, Tavistock Abbey, a prominent Benedictine monastery, played a crucial role in the region's religious and economic life until the 16th-century dissolution.

Cultural Significance:
1. Explore the ruins of the abbey, including the iconic Abbey Chapel.
2. The abbey's dissolution led to the establishment of Tavistock as a market town.
3. The Guildhall, constructed with materials from the abbey, stands as a legacy reminder.

5. Dartmouth Castle - Dartmouth

Guarding the entrance to the Dart Estuary since the 14th century, Dartmouth Castle is a testament to Dartmouth's maritime history and regional defense strategies.

Cultural Significance:
1. Enjoy panoramic views of the estuary from the castle's battlements.
2. Learn about the castle's role in defending against naval threats.
3. Visit the Church of St. Petrox, adjacent to the castle, with its historic charm.

Museums and Art Galleries

Devon's dynamic arts and culture scene showcases the region's creativity and historical richness. Immerse yourself in the diverse array of talent, both local and international, contributing to Devon's vibrant cultural tapestry through these museums and art galleries.

1. Exeter's Royal Albert Memorial Museum (RAMM)

The Royal Albert Memorial Museum, nestled in the heart of Exeter, is a cultural gem encompassing art, archaeology, and natural history. Housed in a historic building, it features a captivating collection reflecting Devon's global connections.

Highlights:
1. Galleries dedicated to world cultures, ancient Egypt, and local history.
2. Contemporary art exhibitions showcasing regional and international artists.
3. Engaging displays on natural history and environmental conservation.

2. Plymouth City Museum and Art Gallery - Plymouth

The Plymouth City Museum and Art Gallery is a dynamic institution celebrating the city's maritime history while offering a comprehensive cultural experience. From archaeological finds to contemporary artworks, this museum showcases a diverse range of artistic expressions.

Highlights:
1. Plymouth Naval and Military Archive featuring maritime artifacts.
2. Collections of fine art, decorative art, and social history.
3. Temporary shows including both local and international artists.

3. Burton Art Gallery and Museum - Bideford

In the charming town of Bideford, the Burton Art Gallery and Museum stands as a cultural hub, blending historical artifacts with contemporary artworks. It plays a crucial role in supporting and promoting local artists.

Highlights:
1. Diverse art collections featuring paintings, sculptures, and crafts.
2. Exhibitions and events supporting emerging and established artists.

3. Educational programs, workshops, and community engagement initiatives.

4. The Art Institute at Plymouth University - Plymouth

The Art Institute at Plymouth University is a dynamic center for contemporary art education and exhibitions. It fosters a creative environment for students and contributes to Plymouth's cultural landscape through innovative artistic endeavors.

Highlights:
1. Student exhibitions showcasing emerging talents.
2. Engaging programs, lectures, and workshops for the public.
3. Collaboration with international artists and institutions.

5. Appledore Crafts Company - Appledore

The Appledore Crafts Company is a cooperative gallery celebrating the work of local artisans and craftspeople in the picturesque village of Appledore. Explore and purchase unique handmade creations.

Highlights:
1. Diverse range of handmade crafts, including ceramics, textiles, and jewelry.

2. rotating exhibitions showcasing the work of local artists.
3. A platform for artists to connect with their peers and visitors.

6. Thelma Hulbert Gallery - Honiton

The Thelma Hulbert Gallery in Honiton is a contemporary art gallery championing the work of local and regional artists. With a focus on contemporary visual arts, the gallery provides a platform for creative exploration and expression.

Highlights:
1. Rotating exhibitions spanning various mediums and artistic styles.
2. Artist-led workshops, talks, and community engagement initiatives.
3. Emphasis on collaboration and supporting emerging talents.

These museums and galleries invite you to immerse yourself in Devon's thriving creative landscape, where history meets innovation and local talent takes center stage.

Entertainment and Nightlife

Devon unfolds a tapestry of delightful entertainment options, ensuring every evening is brimming with memorable experiences. From captivating theaters to vibrant nightlife districts and special events, here's your guide to the diverse entertainment scene in Devon.

1. Theatre Royal - Plymouth

The Theatre Royal in Plymouth stands as a cultural beacon, hosting a wide range of performances, from classic plays to contemporary productions. With a history dating back to the 18th century, the theatre is a cornerstone of the city's artistic heritage.

Highlights:
1. Diverse lineup including dramas, musicals, and ballet performances.
2. Behind-the-scenes tours providing insights into the theater's history.
3. programs that are entertaining for kids and adults alike.

2. Exeter Corn Exchange - Exeter

The Exeter Corn Exchange is a versatile venue hosting a variety of events, including live music, comedy shows, and theatrical performances. With a central location in Exeter, it serves as a cultural hub for locals and visitors.

Highlights:
1. Live music concerts featuring local and touring artists.
2. Comedy nights with stand-up performances from renowned comedians.
3. Dance performances and theatrical productions.

3. Pavilions Teignmouth - Teignmouth

Pavilions Teignmouth offers a diverse entertainment experience, from live music concerts to family-friendly events. Located in the charming seaside town of Teignmouth, the venue provides a picturesque setting for a night out.

Highlights:
1. Live music performances spanning various genres.
2. Family-friendly events, including children's theater and workshops.
3. Cinema screenings and film events.

4. Exeter Quayside Nightlife

As night falls, Exeter's historic quayside transforms into a lively hub of activity. The quayside offers a diverse range of bars, pubs, and entertainment venues, creating a vibrant nightlife scene along the picturesque River Exe.

Highlights:
- Riverside bars and pubs with scenic views of the river.
- Live music performances in atmospheric settings.
- Quirky venues and themed bars for unique experiences.

5. Totnes Folk and Acoustic Nights - Totnes

Totnes is renowned for its eclectic music scene, and the Totnes Folk and Acoustic Nights capture the essence of this musical diversity. These events showcase local and regional folk and acoustic talents in an intimate and welcoming setting.

Highlights:
- Live folk and acoustic performances by emerging and established artists.
- Open mic events offer a forum for local musicians.
- Engaging audience participation and a community atmosphere.

CHAPTER 7
OUTDOOR ADVENTURE AND NATURAL WONDERS

Hikes & Trails in Devon

Devon's various landscapes provide a refuge for hikers, with a myriad of paths catering to all skill levels and interests. Whether you're looking for seaside views, rolling moorlands, or forested valleys, Devon's hiking and path alternatives will captivate your adventurous spirit.

1. South West Coast Path: Coastal Majesty
The South West Coast Path follows the whole Devon coastline, providing stunning views of the craggy cliffs, sandy bays, and azure oceans. This

long-distance path spans 600 miles and lets hikers enjoy the county's coastline splendor at their speed.

Highlights:
1. Visit the UNESCO-listed Jurassic Coast, where fossil-rich cliffs tell the narrative of ancient history.
2. Lundy Island: Take a diversion to Lundy Island for a unique trekking experience and a chance to see seals and seagulls.

2. Dartmoor National Park: Moorland Magic
Dartmoor, with its granite tors and vast moorlands, is a hiking paradise with paths suitable for all levels. Dartmoor's various landscapes, ranging from peaceful walks to strenuous excursions, highlight the raw beauty of the Devon interior.

Highlights:
1. Haytor Rocks Climb Haytor Rocks for stunning views of the moorlands and surrounding countryside.
2. Wistman's Wood: Discover the old and magical Wistman's Wood, complete with moss-covered granite rocks and twisted oaks.

3. Exmoor National Park: Coastal and Countryside Harmony

Exmoor National Park, located on the boundary between Devon and Somerset, is a beautiful combination of coastal cliffs and woodland valleys. Hikers may explore the large network of paths, passing through different landscapes and attractive settlements.

Highlights:
1. Valley of Rocks: Explore the breathtaking Valley of Rocks, a geological wonder with towering cliffs and distinctive rock formations.
2. Tarr Steps: Cross the antique clapper bridge and meander down the river in a peaceful rural environment.

4. Tarka Trail: Riverside Rambling

The Tarka Trail, named after the renowned otter from Henry Williamson's story, offers a picturesque path over old railway lines and riverbanks. This multi-use route encourages hikers to enjoy North Devon's stunning scenery.

Highlights:
1. Riverside Walks: Take leisurely walks along the Taw and Torridge rivers among lush foliage.

2. Bideford to Great Torrington: Traverse the ancient railway route, taking in the pastoral beauty of North Devon.

National and County Parks

Devon's National and County Parks are conserved havens, each offering its combination of natural beauty, historical value, and recreational activities. Immerse yourself in these protected areas, where the magnificence of Devon's landscapes emerges.

1. Dartmoor National Park: Granite Tors and Open Spaces.
Dartmoor is a well-known National Park in the UK, with moorland, old woods, and granite tors. Dartmoor, rich in history and abounding with species, serves as a harsh playground for outdoor lovers.

Highlights:
1. Wild Ponies: See the distinctive Dartmoor ponies grazing freely on the moorlands.
2. Princetown: Visit the settlement of Princetown, which is home to the historic Dartmoor Prison and tourist center.

2. Exmoor National Park: Coastal Tranquility and Moorland Majesty.

Exmoor National Park, which stretches across Devon and Somerset, is a kaleidoscope of landscapes, from heather-covered moorlands to stunning coastal cliffs. This park effortlessly blends natural beauty and cultural history.

Highlights:
1. Dunster Castle: Explore Dunster Castle, set on a hill with views of the Bristol Channel.
2. Tarr steps: Marvel at the old Tarr Steps, a clapper bridge from the Middle Ages.

3. Blackdown Hills AONB: Rolling Countryside Bliss

The Blackdown Hills, which are designated as an Area of Outstanding Natural Beauty (AONB), provide a tranquil getaway among undulating hills, old woods, and picturesque towns. This hidden gem is ideal for people seeking tranquility.

Highlights:
1. Culm Grasslands: Explore this uncommon and vital environment that supports diverse animals.
2. The Wellington Monument: Admire the Wellington Monument, a stunning

monument that offers sweeping views of the surrounding landscape.

4. Plymbridge Woods: Riverside Retreat
Plymbridge Woods is a county park located along the River Plym that offers a variety of forest hikes and riverfront pathways. This accessible getaway is ideal for a family outing or a calm respite from city life.

Highlights:
- The Plym Valley Railway path is a flat and family-friendly route along the river.
- Wildlife Watching: Keep a look out for kingfishers, otters, and other bird species along the riverside.

Water Activities in Devon.

Devon's large coastline, rivers, and lakes offer a playground for water enthusiasts. Devon provides a wide selection of aquatic pleasures, from exhilarating water sports to relaxing river excursions.

1. Surfing in North Devon: Ride the Atlantic Waves
North Devon's shoreline, notably at Croyde Bay and Woolacombe, is a surfing hotspot. With continuous

Atlantic waves, this location draws surfers of all skill levels, from novices to seasoned wave riders.

Highlights:
1. Croyde Bay: Enjoy the big waves at Croyde Bay, noted for its dependable surf breaks.
2. Surfing Schools: Enroll at one of the many surf schools around the shore to receive training and rent equipment.

2. Dartmoor's Wild Swimming: Natural Pools and Waterfalls.
Dartmoor's rivers and natural lakes provide a unique chance for wild swimming. The crystal-clear waters and breathtaking scenery provide for an engaging and pleasant aquatic activity.

Highlights:
1. Discover Sharrah Pool, a remote and lovely place on the Dart River for a peaceful dip.
2. Dartmoor Waterfalls: Explore Dartmoor's waterfalls, such as Becky Falls, and combine a waterfall trek with a refreshing plunge.

3. River Exe Cruises: Serenity on the Water
Take a leisurely boat down the River Exe, where serenity meets magnificent beauty. River Exe cruises provide a pleasant opportunity to enjoy the scenery and see animals along the riverbanks.

Highlights:
1. Exeter Canal and Quays: Take a boat ride down the Exeter Canal, passing through ancient quays and the city center.
2. Avocet Cruises: Join Avocet Cruises for a guided tour, which provides insights into the local History and animals of the River Exe.

4. Coasteering in South Devon: An Adrenaline-Packed Adventure

Coasteering along South Devon's rugged coastlines is an exciting experience for anyone looking for an adrenaline rush. For an exciting aquatic adventure, traverse cliffs, dive into the water, and discover secret tunnels.

Highlights: -1
1. Explore Wembury Bay's craggy shoreline while cliff jumping.
2. Experienced Guides Choose guided coasteering courses with qualified instructors for a safe and entertaining journey.

Wildlife Watching in Devon.

Devon's various environments, from coastal cliffs to vast moorlands, provide a safe home for species. Whether you're a bird watcher, a marine animal lover, or simply enjoy the beauties of nature, Devon's wildlife-watching options will leave you amazed.

1. Lundy Island: Puffins and Seabirds Spectacular
Lundy Island, off the North Devon coast, is a nature lover's dream. The island's cliffs support numerous seabird populations, including puffins, guillemots, and razorbills.

Highlights:
1. Observe seals, dolphins, and basking sharks in the seas surrounding Lundy Island.
2. Guided tours: Join a guided wildlife excursion to increase your chances of seeing Lundy's rich species.

2. Berry Head National Nature Reserve: Coastal BirdWatching
Berry Head, located on the South Devon coast, is a designated National Nature Reserve featuring magnificent cliffs and abundant birds. It provides a fantastic viewpoint for birdwatchers.

Highlights:
1. Peregrine Falcons: Witness the breathtaking displays of peregrine falcons hunting along the cliffs.
2. The Seaview Café: Enjoy birding from the Seaview Café, which is positioned on the cliff with panoramic views.

3 Dawlish Warren Nature Reserve: Wetland Wonders

Dawlish Warren Nature Reserve, located on a sand spit, provides a sanctuary for wetland animals. Birdwatchers can see a wide diversity of birds in this vital coastal environment.

Highlights:
1. Explore the reserve's various habitats, including as mudflats and dunes.
2. Winter waders: Visit during the winter to witness a variety of wading species, including avocets and dunlins.

4. Slapton Ley Nature Reserve: Freshwater Haven

Slapton Ley, the biggest natural lake in South West England, provides a freshwater habitat for species. The reserve, which is surrounded by reedbeds and forests, is home to a diverse range of bird and animal species.

Highlights:
1. Look for otters and kingfishers along Slapton Ley's shoreline.
2. Walking Trails: Visit the reserve's walking trails to see dragonflies, butterflies, and a variety of wildlife.

Scenic Drives In Devon

Devon's stunning vistas and meandering roads make it an excellent choice for scenic drives. Whether you're driving along seaside cliffs, meandering through charming villages, or rising moorland heights, these gorgeous routes highlight the region's rich splendor.

1. North Devon Coastal Route: Seaside Splendor
The North Devon Coastal Route follows the rough coastline, providing panoramic vistas of cliffs, sandy beaches, and picturesque settlements. This picturesque trip is a visual feast for those who like the splendor of the Atlantic.

Highlights:
1. Explore Clovelly, a timeless town with cobblestone streets and a gorgeous harbor.
2. Hartland Peninsula: Hartland Quay offers magnificent cliffside vistas and unusual rock formations.

2. Dartmoor's High Moorland Drive: Granite Tors and Open Vistas

The High Moorland Drive takes you deep into Dartmoor's nature. This road, winding past granite tors and wide expanses, immerses you in the moor's distinctive sceneries.

Highlights:
1. From Princetown to Postbridge: Travel from Princetown to Postbridge over Dartmoor's high moorland, including Tavistock and Burrator Reservoirs.
2. Explore the market town of Tavistock and take a lovely drive around Burrator Reservoir.

3. The Jurassic Coast Road Trip: Fossil-Adorned Beauty

Take a road trip along the Jurassic Coast, a UNESCO World Heritage Site. This path provides breathtaking views of East Devon's historic landscapes, fossil-rich beaches, and towering cliffs.

Highlights:
1. Drive from Sidmouth to Lyme Regis through gorgeous coastal villages.
2. Lyme Regis Fossil Beach Explore Lyme Regis and its famed fossil beaches, a popular

destination for fossil seekers and beachcombers.

4. South Devon Coast Drive: Estuaries and Secluded Coves

The South Devon Coastal Drive follows the scenic coastline, displaying estuaries, sandy bays, and secret coves. This journey highlights the gentler side of Devon's seaside beauty.

Highlights:
1. Salcombe Estuary Enjoy views of the Salcombe Estuary, which is recognized for its sailing tradition and picturesque beauty.
2. Starting Bay and Slapton Sands: Drive around Start Bay, stopping at Slapton Sands for a relaxing beach experience.

5. Exmoor's Coastal and Countryside Loop: Variety of Landscapes

Explore Exmoor's many vistas with a beach and rural loop. This route takes you through heather-covered moorlands, quaint towns, and along the jagged coastline.

Highlights:
1. Lynton and Lynmouth. Visit the twin communities of Lynton and Lynmouth, linked by a cliff railway.

2. The Valley of Rocks: Drive through the Valley of Rocks, a breathtaking natural amphitheater with wild goats and coastline vistas.

CHAPTER 8
SHOPPING AND SOUVENIR

Unique Devon Souvenirs

Devon's allure is not limited to its scenery; it permeates even the souvenirs made there. Every location, from charming seaside towns to ancient villages, provides one-of-a-kind mementos that perfectly embody Devon. Think about these essential mementos:

Pottery Made by Hand:
Devon has a long history of producing exquisite ceramics. Bring a bit of its history home with you with hand-thrown ceramics that have vivid glazes and detailed patterns. You can discover a unique ceramic masterpiece at locations like the Devon Guild of Craftsmen, which highlights the skills of regional craftspeople.

Jewelry with a Sea Theme:
Wear jewelry that is inspired by the sea to embrace the seaside vibes. Devon's seaside villages are home to boutique jewelers who craft exquisite items that capture the beauty of the water, ranging from tiny seashell necklaces to nautical-themed bracelets.

These classic pieces will bring back memories of your trips by the water.

Prints of Local Art:
Using locally created art prints, you can bring the beauty of Devon's landscapes inside your house. The breathtaking landscape is often depicted on canvas or paper by local artists. Seek prints featuring the magnificent cliffs along the Jurassic Coast, the undulating landscapes of Exmoor, or the tors of Dartmoor.

Tea Kits with Devonshire Cream:
Consider taking home a Cream Tea kit as a delectable reminder of Devon's culinary history. With these kits, you can replicate the popular Devonshire Cream Tea experience in the comfort of your own home. They are packaged with locally produced clotted cream, jam, and scone mix.

Local Spirits and Devon Gin:
In recent years, Devon's craft gin sector has grown significantly. Visit the area's distilleries and return with a bottle of handcrafted gin blended with local botanicals. You may take guided tours of some distilleries to see the distillation process in action.

Local Markets and Shopping Districts

Devon offers more to discover than just its scenic attractions; its thriving marketplaces and retail centers offer a window into everyday life. The markets in Devon provide something for everyone, whether you're looking for locally produced goods, handcrafted items, or distinctive clothing.

Market: Totnes:

Totnes Market is a veritable gold mine of handcrafted items, tucked away in the center of South Devon. Handcrafted jewelry and organic vegetables abound, creating a bohemian appeal in the market atmosphere. Don't pass up the opportunity to engage with regional craftsmen and do some eco-friendly shopping.

Gandy Street, Exeter:

Enter Exeter's Gandy Street, a picturesque cobblestone street brimming with individual stores and quaint cafés. This colorful street has a variety of antique goods, custom apparel, and unusual presents. It's the ideal location to explore and find undiscovered treasures.

North Devon's Pannier Markets:

North Devon's Pannier Markets are a great place to see the area's agricultural skills in action. Handmade goods, antiques, and fresh local fruit are all available at these lively markets. The Pannier Market in Bideford is especially well-known for its wide selection of goods.

Foss Street in Dartmouth:
Foss Street in Dartmouth is a charming retail area with a nautical theme. Visit boutiques that sell handcrafted chocolates and clothing with a seaside vibe. The place is a lovely place for leisurely shopping because of its beautiful environment.

Royal William Yard, Plymouth:
Visit the Royal William Yard in Plymouth for a distinctive shopping experience. Formerly a military victualing yard, this area is now home to chic shops, galleries, and seaside eateries. Take pleasure in shopping while admiring the breathtaking marine architecture.

Crafts & Arts

Devon's creative heritage is as varied as its topography. Discovering the works of the county's flourishing artistic and craftsman sector reveals the genuine essence of Devon's inventive spirit.

Bovey Tracey, Devon Guild of Craftsmen):

The Devon Guild of Craftsmen, located in Bovey Tracey, was established in 1955 and is a refuge for those who enjoy modern workmanship. The guild features a wide variety of handcrafted goods, such as jewelry, woodworking, textiles, and pottery. Buy a one-of-a-kind item straight from the creators to help the regional craft scene.

Torrington's Dartington Crystal:

Devon is known for its exquisite crystal work, with Torrington's Dartington Crystal leading the way. Discover the glassblowing process at the tourist center and shop, where you can also select from an exquisite selection of crystal glassware, such as sophisticated wine glasses and ornamental pieces.

Craft Workshops at Buckland Abbey:

Formerly the residence of Sir Francis Drake, Buckland Abbey today offers artisan programs that let guests get fully immersed in traditional skills. Take part in painting, weaving, or pottery classes to produce a work of art inspired by Devon that you can bring home.

Salcombe's Coastal Art Galleries:

Salcombe, with its spectacular views of the seaside, has developed into a refuge for artists. Discover the town's art galleries, which include prints, sculptures, and paintings with a maritime theme. The sea inspires a lot of artists, who use it to convey the spirit of Devon's seaside charm.

Textiles and Devonshire Lace:
Devon is known for its lace-making legacy, which is commemorated in several workshops and studios. Visit locations like Branscombe Lace Workshop to see the elaborate process of creating lace, or look for locally produced textile art that tells tales.

Antique Stores

Devon's antique stores are a charming part of its historic district, where you may find unique items from bygone times. Devon's antique stores provide a trip down memory lane for both novice and expert collectors.

Exeter's Topsham Antiques:
Topsham Antiques is located just outside of Exeter in the quaint town of Topsham. This group of vendors has a wide selection of vintage jewelry, collectibles, and furniture. Explore its carefully chosen exhibits to find one-of-a-kind items with intriguing backstories.

Cider Press Centre Dartington's (Totnes):

The Cider Press Centre, tucked away in the Dartington estate close to Totnes, offers more than simply cider. Discover its artisan stores, which offer vintage and antique items. The institution frequently holds antique fairs where visitors may browse a large assortment of classic items.

Lynmouth's Antique Complex:

Enthusiasts of collecting might find the Antique Complex in the charming hamlet of Lynmouth. This multi-dealer store has an amazing selection of antiquities, including pottery and furniture. A visit here mixes the excitement of exploration with breathtaking scenery because of its proximity to the magnificent Exmoor National Park.

Antiques from the Tavistock Pannier Market:

The Pannier Market is a must-see for visitors to Tavistock, a quaint market town. There are days when antique vendors set up shop in the market, selling an amazing selection of old clothes and furnishings.

Dulverton's Exmoor Antiques:

Antique lovers are drawn to Exmoor Antiques, which is located near Dulverton on the border of Exmoor. A selection of timeless objects, vintage fabrics, and antique cutlery are among the carefully chosen items in this charming store. The attractive surroundings enhance the appeal of your treasure quest.

Devon's retail scene is a fascinating fusion of modernity and heritage. Discovering ageless gems in antique stores, perusing through ancient marketplaces, or getting lost in local crafts—each encounter provides a different perspective on Devon's diverse cultural landscape. You will take with you the stories of Devon's landscapes and the creative energy that characterizes this wonderful county as you return home with keepsakes, artistic works, and antique treasures.

CHAPTER 9
ITINERARY

Short Stay Itinerary (2 Days)

Day 1: Coastal Charms in Torquay

8:00 AM - 10:00 AM: Morning Delights
- Begin your day in Torquay, the English Riviera.
- Savor breakfast with a sea view at The Singing Kettle.
- Take a stroll along Torre Abbey Sands.

12:00 PM - 2:00 PM: Seafood Sensations
- Indulge in seafood delights at Pier Point Restaurant.
- Explore Living Coasts marine zoo for an aquatic adventure.
- Enjoy picturesque views along Princess Pier.

6:00 PM - 8:00 PM: Evening Elegance
- Dine at The Elephant, a Michelin-starred restaurant.
- Conclude your evening with a show at the Princess Theatre or a seaside nightcap.

Day 2: Dartmoor National Park Discovery

8:00 AM - 10:00 AM: Journey to Dartmoor
- Head to Dartmoor National Park, a rugged landscape.
- Breakfast at Fox Tor Café on the park's edge.
- Visit Haytor, an iconic granite tor, for panoramic views.

12:00 PM - 2:00 PM: Picnic in the Park
- Enjoy a picnic lunch surrounded by stunning Dartmoor landscapes.
- Explore Becky Falls, a beautiful waterfall nestled in Dartmoor.
- Drive through winding roads, savoring the beauty of the park.

6:00 PM - 8:00 PM: Dartmoor Evening
- Dinner at The Rugglestone Inn, a traditional Dartmoor pub.
- Relax and stargaze in the clear Dartmoor night sky.

Medium Stay Itinerary (5 Days)

Day 1: Cultural Immersion in Exeter

9:00 AM - 11:00 AM: Explore Exeter's Heritage
- Arrive in Exeter and enjoy breakfast at Tea on the Green.
- Give yourself a thorough historical education at Exeter Cathedral.

1:00 PM - 3:00 PM: Art and Lunch
- Lunch at The Real Food Store, known for locally sourced delights.
- Visit the Royal Albert Memorial Museum for art and history.
- Stroll along the historic Quayside, absorbing the city's cultural vibe.

7:00 PM - 9:00 PM: Evening in Exeter
- Dine at The White Hart, a historic pub with modern flair.
- Attend a performance at Exeter Phoenix, experiencing the city's artistic side.

Day 2: Coastal Retreat in Sidmouth

8:00 AM - 10:00 AM: Journey to Sidmouth
- Drive to Sidmouth, a charming coastal town.
- Breakfast with sea views at Dukes café.
- Explore the Connaught Gardens, showcasing coastal flora.

12:00 PM - 2:00 PM: Coastal Cuisine
- Lunch at The Pea Green Boat Café, savoring coastal cuisine.
- Afternoon stroll along the charming promenade and Sidmouth Beach.

7:00 PM - 9:00 PM: Evening Relaxation
- Dinner at The Salty Monk, a historic inn with a gourmet touch.
- Unwind in the tranquility of Sidmouth, enjoying the coastal breeze.

Day 3: Seaside Bliss in Salcombe

9:00 AM - 11:00 AM: Arrival in Salcombe
- Journey to Salcombe, a charming seaside town.
- Breakfast at The Winking Prawn, a beachfront gem.
- Explore Salcombe Maritime Museum for maritime history.

1:00 PM - 3:00 PM: Sailing and Coastal Views
- Lunch at The Crab Shed, indulging in fresh seafood.
- Enjoy an afternoon boat trip for Salcombe's coastal views.
- Relax at North Sands beach, away from the bustling town.

7:00 PM - 9:00 PM: Sunset Dining
- Dine at The Victoria Inn, a cozy pub with warmth.
- Watch the sunset over Salcombe estuary, a picturesque end.

Day 4: Nature and Tranquility in Totnes

8:00 AM - 10:00 AM: Journey to Totnes
- Drive to Totnes, a riverside market town.
- Breakfast at Waterside Bistro, with scenic river views.
- Visit historic Totnes Castle for medieval insights.

12:00 PM - 2:00 PM: Riverside Lunch
- Lunch at The Steam Packet Inn, a relaxed riverside pub.
- Stroll along the River Dart, enjoying the peaceful surroundings.

- Explore Totnes' independent shops and markets for unique finds.

7:00 PM - 9:00 PM: Totnes Evening
- Dinner at The Wild Fig, known for its creative menu.
- Attend a performance at Totnes Cinema or relax in local pubs.

Day 5: Farewell in Plymouth

9:00 AM - 11:00 AM: Arrival in Plymouth
- Travel to Plymouth, a historic maritime city.
- Breakfast at The Column Bakehouse in Royal William Yard.
- Explore the Mayflower Steps and the Royal Citadel.

1:00 PM - 3:00 PM: Maritime Exploration
- Lunch at The Dock, a waterfront restaurant.
- Visit The National Marine Aquarium for a marine adventure.
- Walk along Hoe Promenade for stunning vistas of Plymouth Sound.

7:00 PM - 9:00 PM: Plymouth Farewell
- Dinner at The Greedy Goose, offering modern British cuisine.

- Reflect on your Devon adventure with a stroll along the Barbican waterfront.

Extended Stay Itinerary (10 Days)

Day 6: Coastal Wonder in Clovelly

9:00 AM - 11:00 AM: Arrival in Clovelly
- Begin your day in the picturesque village of Clovelly, celebrated for its cobbled streets.
- Enjoy a hearty breakfast at The Red Lion, a charming inn with scenic sea views.
- Explore the historic village, renowned for its preserved, traffic-free ambiance.

1:00 PM - 3:00 PM: Maritime Cuisine and Views
- Savor a seafood-infused lunch at New Inn.
- Take a scenic stroll along the South West Coast Path, offering breathtaking views.
- Visit Clovelly Harbour and delve into the village's seafaring history.

7:00 PM - 9:00 PM: Dinner with Ocean Breeze
- Dine at The Harbour Lights, relishing a meal with the soothing sound of waves.
- Experience the tranquility of Clovelly as the evening unfolds.

Day 7: Riverside Serenity in Lynmouth

8:00 AM - 10:00 AM: Journey to Lynmouth
- Drive to Lynmouth, a coastal town nestled at the confluence of the East and West Lyn rivers.
- Breakfast at The Pavilion Dining Room, offering picturesque river views.
- Embark on a scenic ride on the Lynton and Lynmouth Cliff Railway for panoramic views.

12:00 PM - 2:00 PM: Waterside Lunch
- Enjoy a leisurely lunch at The Rising Sun, a historic inn with a riverside terrace.
- Explore the serene Watersmeet, where the rivers converge amidst lush greenery.
- Stroll along Lynmouth Beach, absorbing the refreshing seaside ambiance.

7:00 PM - 9:00 PM: Evening by the River
- Dine at The Ancient Mariner, a riverside restaurant with a cozy ambiance.
- Immerse yourself in the tranquil atmosphere of Lynmouth as night falls.

Day 8: Moorland Magic in Tavistock

9:00 AM - 11:00 AM: Arrival in Tavistock
- Travel to Tavistock, a market town on the edge of Dartmoor.
- Begin your day with breakfast at The Cornish Arms, a traditional pub exuding warmth.
- Explore Tavistock's historic market and the charming Pannier Market.

1:00 PM - 3:00 PM: Cultural Exploration
- Savor lunch at The Bedford Hotel, a historic coaching inn.
- Visit Tavistock Abbey and immerse yourself in its medieval history.
- Stroll along the scenic River Tavy, appreciating the town's riverside charm.

7:00 PM - 9:00 PM: Dinner in Town
- Conclude your day with dinner at The Taylors, offering modern British cuisine in a stylish setting.
- Soak in the evening ambiance of Tavistock.

Day 9-10: Personal Exploration and Relaxation

These two days are intentionally left flexible for personal exploration—whether revisiting favorite spots, discovering hidden gems, or simply relishing the serene surroundings of Devon. Consider activities like hiking, exploring local markets, or indulging in spa treatments for a truly personalized experience.

Reflecting on Your Devon Odyssey

As your extended stay in Devon concludes, take a moment to reflect on the diverse experiences, scenic landscapes, and rich history you've encountered. Whether you chose the short, medium, or extended itinerary, Devon has undoubtedly left an indelible mark on your travel memories.

CHAPTER 10
SAFETY, HEALTH TIPS, AND FIRST AID

Travel Safety Tips

Welcome to Devon, where scenic landscapes and quaint villages await your exploration. To make the most of your journey, follow these safety tips for a seamless and secure adventure:

1. Weather-Ready Wardrobe:
   - Tip: Pack layers for unpredictable weather, especially along the coast.

2. Road Wisdom:
   - Tip: Drive cautiously on narrow rural roads; understand local traffic rules.

3. Coastal Caution:
   - Tip: Mind tides and currents at the beaches; adhere to safety guidelines.

4. Wildlife Respect:
   - Tip: Keep a safe distance from wildlife; obey signs indicating their presence.

5. Emergency Essentials:
   - Tip: Save local emergency numbers; know nearby medical and police facilities.

6. Sturdy Steps:
   - Tip: Wear sturdy footwear for trails; some areas have uneven terrain.

7. Sun Savvy:
   - Tip: Apply sunscreen even on cloudy days; don a hat and sunglasses.

8. Local Know-How:
   - Tip: Stay informed about local guidelines, especially during peak seasons.

9. Culinary Caution:
   - Tip: Relish local cuisine safely; choose reputable eateries, especially for seafood.

10. Digital Vigilance:
    - Tip: Secure belongings; use trusted Wi-Fi; be cautious online.

Embark on your Devon adventure confidently, balancing tranquility with coastal excitement.

Health Precautions

A healthy journey enhances your Devon experience. Whether exploring cities, moors, or coastal havens, these health precautions ensure your well-being:

1. Vaccine Vigilance:
   - Precaution: Keep routine and travel-specific vaccinations up-to-date.

2. Insured and Assured:
   - Precaution: Prioritize medical emergency coverage in travel insurance.

3. Hydration Headquarters:
   - Precaution: Stay hydrated with a reusable bottle, crucial for diverse landscapes.

4. Bite and Sting Safeguard:
   - Precaution: Use insect repellent in certain areas; guard against ticks and mosquitoes.

5. Sunshield Strategies:
   - Precaution: Shield against the sun; apply sunscreen, wear protective clothing.

6. Medicine Mastery:
   - Precaution: Pack necessary medications and a basic first aid kit.

7. Local Lifelines:
   - Precaution: Know the locations of local healthcare services; save emergency numbers.

8. Eats and Drinks Caution:
   - Precaution: Consume food and beverages wisely; prioritize hygiene.

9. Restful Rendezvous:
   - Precaution: Prioritize sufficient rest for an enjoyable travel experience.

10. Pandemic Preparedness:
    - Precaution: Stay updated on travel advisories and adhere to COVID-19 protocols.

11. Hiking Happiness:
    - Precaution: Care for your feet during extensive hikes with suitable footwear.

12. Fit and Fun Activities:
    - Precaution: Choose activities aligned with your fitness level.

Enjoy Devon fully by integrating these health precautions into your travel plans.

Emergency Contacts

While Devon promises safety, be prepared with these essential emergency contacts:

1. Emergency Services:
   - Contact: **999 or 112**

Note: Immediate assistance for police, fire, ambulance, or emergencies.

2. Non-Emergency Police:
   - Contact: **101**

Note: For non-urgent incidents or general police advice.

3. Medical Emergencies:
   - Contact: NHS **111**

Note: Medical advice for non-life-threatening emergencies.

4. Coastguard:
   - Contact: 999 or 112 (Ask for Coastguard)

Note: Coastal emergencies, water rescues, maritime incidents.

5. Mountain Rescue:
   - Contact: 999 or 112 (Ask for Mountain Rescue)

Note: Incidents in hilly terrains, especially Dartmoor or Exmoor.

6. First Aid Assistance:
- Contact: British Red Cross - 0344 871 11 11

Note: First aid advice and assistance.

7. Document Dilemmas:
- Contact: Local Police Station

Note: Report lost or stolen documents, passports, valuables.

8. Consulate Connections:

Contact: Check with your home country's embassy or consulate.

Note: Assistance for serious emergencies related to nationality.

First Aid Essentials

Prepare for minor hiccups with a well-packed first aid kit tailored for Devon's adventures:

1. Wound Wonderland:

Items:
- Sterile dressings, band-aids, antiseptic wipes, tweezers, scissors.

2. Pain-Relief Parade:
Items:
- Paracetamol or ibuprofen, pain relief ointment or gel.

3. Digestive Defense:
Items:
- Antacids, anti-diarrheal meds, rehydration sachets.

4. Allergy Armor:
Items:
- Antihistamine tablets or cream, insect repellent, bite relief cream.

5. Medication Must-Haves:
Items:
- Ample supply of prescription meds; list of meds and dosages.

6. Sun Safeguard:
Items:
- Sunscreen, aloe vera gel for sunburn relief.

7. Foot Care Fiesta:
Items:
- Blister plasters, foot powder, or anti-chafing balm.

8. Toolbox Essentials:
Items:
- Small scissors, tweezers for splinter removal, safety pins.

9. Hygiene Haven:
Items:
- Hand sanitizer, wet wipes, and personal hygiene items.

10. Emergency Info Arsenal:
Items:
- List of emergency contacts, travel insurance details copy.

11. Tech Tactics:
Items:
- Portable charger, emergency whistle, or signal mirror.

12. Document Defense:
Items:
- Photocopies of important documents, a printed list of emergency contacts.

13. Compact First Aid Wisdom:
Items:
- Small first aid manual for reference.

14. Specialized Care (if needed):
Items:
- EpiPen for severe allergies, inhaler for respiratory conditions.

CONCLUSION

Thank you for embarking on this journey through the pages of "Discover Devon: A Travel Guide." We appreciate your choice to make our guidebook your companion in exploring the captivating landscapes and cultural richness of Devon.

As your guide through this enchanting region, we aim to offer a curated experience that blends coastal charms, countryside retreats, and historic gems. From the vibrant city life of Exeter to the tranquil shores of Torquay, the rugged beauty of Dartmoor, and the timeless villages like Clovelly and Lynmouth, Devon has unfolded its diverse tapestry for you to explore.

Throughout these pages, we've provided insights into the regions, must-visit attractions, diverse accommodation options, and a taste of the local culinary scene. Our itineraries were designed to cater to varying preferences, ensuring that whether your stay is short, medium, or extended, Devon's wonders are at your fingertips.

Remember, Devon is more than a destination; it's an invitation to immerse yourself in history, embrace natural beauty, and savor the warmth of its communities. As you venture into the charming towns, explore coastal wonders, and meander through the moors, may the experiences captured in this guidebook become treasured moments in your travel story.

Devon's allure lies not only in its landscapes but also in the memories you'll create as you traverse its paths. Whether you find solace in the seaside retreats, marvel at historic landmarks, or simply enjoy the warmth of a Devonshire cream tea, we hope this guide has enriched your travel experience.

Once again, thank you for choosing "Discover Devon: A Travel Guide." May your exploration of this remarkable region be filled with discovery, joy, and a lasting connection to the essence of Devon. Safe travels, and may your Devon adventure be as unique and memorable as the landscapes you'll encounter.

Printed in Great Britain
by Amazon